10 Rules to Survive the Internet Dating Jungle

2nd Book in The Dating Jungle Series

By Tara Richter

Editor Casey Cavanagh

Published by Richter Publishing LLC

www.richterpublishing.com

Copyright 2013 by Tara Richter & The Dating Jungle

ISBN-10:069262225X
ISBN-13:9780692622254

DEDICATION

I would like to dedicate my second dating book to all my friends who have given me some great stories to share within these pages. To my editor Casey for putting in some grueling hours over the holidays. To all the wacky bad internet dates I've been on. To all the interesting emails and user profiles I was able to view. Within doing this kind of research there never is a dull moment. Some profiles made me laugh, some made me cringe and others made me scared.

CONTENTS

DISCLAIMER

This book is designed to provide information on dating only. This information is provided and sold with the knowledge that the publisher and author do not offer any legal or medical advice. In the case of a need for any such expertise consult with the appropriate professional. This book does not contain all information available on the subject. This book has not been created to be specific to any individual's or organizations' situation or needs. Every effort has been made to make this book as accurate as possible. However, there may be typographical and or content errors. Therefore, this book should serve only as a general guide and not as the ultimate source of subject information. This book contains information that might be dated and is intended only to educate and entertain. The author and publisher shall have no liability or responsibility to any person or entity regarding any loss or damage incurred, or alleged to have incurred, directly or indirectly, by the information contained in this book. You hereby agree to be bound by this disclaimer or you may return this book within the guarantee time period for a full refund.

In the interest of full disclosure, this book contains affiliate links that might pay the author or publisher a commission upon any purchase from the company. While the author and publisher take no responsibility for the business practices of these companies and or the performance of any product or service, the author or publisher has used the product or service and makes a recommendation in good faith based on that experience.

All characters appearing in this work are fictitious. Any resemblance to real persons, living or dead, is purely coincidental.

INTRODUCTION

When I told my mother I was going to be doing my first ever television interview with Daytime TV, her first question was "Well why do they want to interview you?" The jab initially hurt, but it got me thinking. *Who am I? Why do syndicated talk shows want to interview me? Why do I deserve to be on television or radio? Yes, I wrote and published a book on dating, but who am I?*

I am you.

I am every woman who has been through divorce, and survived.

Who am I? I'm every woman who's been through a toxic relationship and had the power to stop it.

I'm every woman who grew up in a divorced family, with an alcoholic father who cheated on their mother, left to pursue his career and didn't come back fully in our lives until I was a teenager.

Who am I? I'm the awkward, overweight, too tall adolescent girl who felt left out and made fun of. I'm the insecure teenager who started doing drugs in high school to lose weight and fit in.

What sets me apart? I've been able to heal my wounds and become fully aware of whom I am. I can fully accept and love myself without approval or acceptance from anyone else.

Now I want to share what I've learned in my journeys and help everyone else get to this happy place in their lives too. Once you're truly happy with yourself, then you can find a healthy relationship. This is my second book that I am publishing about dating. Obviously, I am a woman and I try to keep my writing from both points of view to help men and women alike. Though, sometimes it's hard since I have only experienced dating from a woman's point of view. Some readers think my books are only for women, but my books can help everyone. It's also not just about dating, it's about how to survive the world and take your life back.

In this edition I am trying even more to get both sexes point of view and information within the dating jungle, since it's vastly different between men and women. In an effort to do so, I conducted interviews of various men who have ventured out into the internet dating jungle. I have picked them from different ages and backgrounds to get a better feel for the males' perspectives. At the end of each chapter is a section "From the Y Chromosome". It will have men's advice, funny dating stories and more. So if you think the dating jungle advice is just for women, think again!

Here's a little background on each of my male interviewees:

Nathan is 28 years old. He is an accountant in Tampa Bay working towards his CPA. He has never been married or have any children. An attractive 6 feet and some change tall, intellectual who is just now getting out into the dating jungle. He focused himself in college to study hard and get good grades, so he didn't participate in the normal bar hopping and parties as most college students do. He's fairly green to relationships and I think his over analytical mind sometimes works against him in his efforts to find the one. A more shy personality he has done a lot of good things to get him out of his own comfort zone to meet people by various activities. Some which include: learning salsa and bachata, attending Pre-Date Speed Dating events, going to men's relationship groups, and of course, utilizing internet dating sites.

Dan is 56 years old and has never been married or have kids. He has a business that he runs with family members. He has vast experience out in the dating jungle yet until now hasn't found his soul-mate. Currently he is in a long term relationship with a younger woman, 37 years old, that he met on Match.com. They live together in his manufactured home and have been dating for 1.5 years. Dan is an

Italian, old fashioned guy. He believes that women shouldn't swear because it's unattractive. He believes he's still young at heart and likes to attend live AC/DC concerts. This is why he wants to be with a younger woman because he believes women his age are boring.

Chris is 41 years old and just recently coming off his second divorce. The tall with rugged good looks divorcee, has no children from either marriage. He is fairly new to the internet dating world and is just starting to test out the various sites. Chris is fairly active in playing sports, like hockey, in various leagues on the weekends. He works as a computer programmer and does other projects on the side such as develop iPhone apps. He is not necessarily happy about being out in the single world and trying to figure all this out again. He's sweet and genuine, yet a little wounded still from his last relationship.

Jerry is 60 years old and has been divorced for 18 years with two daughters. He is a lawyer in the Tampa Bay area and also enjoys participating in live theatrical performances. Very intelligent and articulate, he knows what he wants, yet had a long time trying to find it. He has been on dating sites since they first came out long time ago. He's been on just about all of them and also utilized other methods such as a Match Maker. Eventually he found his angel on Match.com and has been in a exclusive relationship with her for about 18 months.

RULE # 1
ARE YOU READY TO DATE?

This is the most important rule in the entire book. It is why I put it before all the others and why it was the first rule in my last book, "10 Rules to Survive the Dating Jungle." I refer to it as "Heal Your Wounds" in the first book, yet they have the same premise in both. I recommend reading the first book before this one. If you have, great! If not, it is very important you master this rule before you go on to any other rule in the book.

Most people decide to start dating because of a break up, divorce or because they are lonely. They take the steps to start dating by putting up an online profile or by having their friends set them up. But rarely do they ever ask themselves if they are *ready* to date. Just because you were recently separated from your significant other does not mean you should start dating right away. Let the ink dry on the divorce papers first. Take some time for yourself.

I had a discussion with one of my readers about being lonely. I honestly think that loneliness is a direct result of not being happy with yourself, which is why you don't enjoy spending time alone. When you are alone all your issues bubble up. If you can't face them, you keep yourself busy to distract from what's really going on by either chatting endlessly on dating sites, drinking, going on bad dates, or hanging out with people you don't enjoy.

Going through a divorce is one of the hardest events that someone can endure in their lifetime. Most often you forget who you are in the process. Getting so wrapped up in the other person's personality, it's possible to lose your special qualities. Take some time off to get to know *you* again. During my marriage I completely lost my creative juices. It was only once I decided to take a year off from life that they started flowing back into me.

I call it taking a year off from life because I quit my 9-5 job, started writing my first book, and didn't date. For the first time in my life, I started to actually feel my emotions. I didn't even know until then I had so many repressed feelings shoved all the way down inside me. Once I completely focused all my energy on myself and stopped worrying about everyone else, I discovered how much emotional baggage I was carrying around.

As has been said many times over, you can't love someone else if you don't love yourself. How can you expect to give someone else love if you can't give it to yourself first? In order to love yourself, you need to heal any emotional wounds that you have endured over your lifetime. These can be any bad relationships in your life--boyfriends, husbands, fathers, brothers, mothers, wives, close friends, et cetera. The first relationships that you develop with your immediate family during adolescence have a huge impact on your dating life and how you perceive an intimate relationship should function. We also develop what our idea of a relationship is and how a man should treat a woman/ woman should treat a man all from ages of three to five years old.

I have this as the first rule in the dating jungle because if you don't start off with a positive place within yourself, none of the other rules will matter. You would only be building the rules on very shaky foundations. If you've been in a string of bad relationships, one after another, you need to start taking a look inside yourself. I did. If you had just one bad relationship and learned from it, that's great. That's how it should be. You realize that's what you *didn't* want in a partner and went for the opposite in another. That is a healthy way to grow and develop.

Maybe you're more like me; I had three major relationships in my life that were pretty much all the same, just different jerks. They might as well have been the same guy with different faces and addresses. The definition of insanity is doing the same thing over and over again and expecting a different result. After my marriage ended I thought I was going insane. I couldn't believe how I kept finding these crazy guys. What was wrong with me? I thought to myself, *I'm attractive, intelligent, and down-to-earth. Why can't I find a normal guy?* I really thought maybe all guys were jerks, or that I deserved to be treated like this. Maybe love just wasn't in the cards for me. It seemed like everything else in my life was perfect, besides finding love.

I didn't realize that I was going out into the dating jungle as damaged goods. I had no idea how much emotional wreckage I was carrying around inside. Once I healed my wounds, I was able to see clearly. Life became positive and fun again. The great thing about emotional wounds is that they are just like physical wounds. If you break your arm and put it in a cast and allow it time to heal, you're good as new. Same goes with the scars on the inside. If you take the time to really cry, scream, be depressed for a while, then eventually your wounds will heal. It takes time, though. It took about a year for me to heal everything. It wasn't just my divorce; it was a lot of issues from my childhood that I had never dealt with. Once I started feeling and crying about one situation, I thought I was good for a month. Then something else would pop up, then a week later something else. I thought it was never going to end, but it finally did.

It will for you, too. One day you will wake up and truly be happy,100 percent happy, not fake happy. You will know when it happens because you will feel it in every cell of your body. From the tips of your toes to the ends of your fingers, you will tingle with excitement. It's the best feeling in the world. I honestly didn't have that feeling until about just a few months ago, (about October 2012). Now I have that feeling all the time because I'm living my life for me, no one else.

I know this is a dating book, but in reality the 10 Rules I composed in this book and the last one can be applied to anything in life. Since I've been implementing my rules, my books have taken off, my businesses are flourishing and life is truly wonderful. I haven't found a serious relationship again, yet I'm having fun being single and enjoying just being me. I would like to get married again, but not anytime soon. Though, all of my relationships have become healthy ones: friendships, dating, and family. Why? Because I won't stand for anything less. I deserve the best from anyone who chooses to be part of my life.

Burning Therapy

This is something I created myself after my divorce, something to help you heal emotional wounds. After you end a relationship there's a lot of left over stuff that lingers and haunts you. Every time you turn a corner you see something that reminds you of your ex. Photos, books, presents, you name it. The longer you two have been together, the more stuff you accumulate. Now the question is, since the relationship is dead, what do you do with all this stuff?

Once my divorce was finalized, instead of being sad and depressed about it, I decided to celebrate the new chapter in my life ahead of me. I hosted a divorce party with all my close friends. This is getting pretty popular now a days. Probably because a lot of people are going through divorce or just want another reason to throw a party!

I had my divorce party at my dad's house on St. Pete Beach. I was living there after my separation since I didn't have anywhere else to go. My ex and I were married for like a second; I think the stain on

Monica Lewinski's dress stayed around longer than our marriage did, so I had tons of wedding stuff. The last thing I wanted to see was left over wedding invites, RSVP cards, and well wishes for the happy couple.

I could have just thrown all that stuff into a garbage can, but what's the fun in that? No, I had to do something different, something that would really allow me to release all the negative energy and bad emotions from my past. Just throwing my marriage in the garbage and putting it out on the curb didn't do justice for the hell my ex put me through—all the pain he caused deep inside my soul and the cracks he created in my heart. No, this deserved a ceremony—a burning ceremony. Thus, burning therapy was born.

The first half of the divorce party was normal: drinks, appetizers, music, and socializing. The second half the burning ceremony began. By this time the sun had already set behind the ocean and the stars were out glistening over the dark intercostal waters. We all gathered around the fire pit and set flames to the wood. Soon, yellow and orange colors danced across the logs. I pulled out left over RSVP cards from the wedding and one by one dropped them into the pit. The corners bursts into flames and the paper curled up. February 27th 2010, our wedding date that was printed on the card slowly melted and disappeared. Soon the entire card was just ashes blowing in the wind.

It felt fantastic! I couldn't wait to burn more stuff. This was the best feeling in the world! With every piece of memory slowly burning away to nothing, so did my pain. The energy of the fire was sucking all the negativity out of my soul. I was mesmerized by the fire, starring into the glowing embers. Each item I burned I felt lighter and lighter. I was sweating profusely from the heat of the flames, but I didn't notice it because I felt indestructible.

Cleansing Places

This is another little tool I devised to utilize for myself and some of my friends to help get over past relationships. This is fun and you can get your friends together to help you. After a relationship is over, bad memories linger like ghosts haunting the places you used to have fun at with that person. Sometimes it's too hard to go back to your favorite restaurant where you had your anniversary dinner. Every time you think of it, memories frolic in your head of the fun you used to have and it becomes too painful to go back. Though, you can't avoid every establishment for the rest of your life, unless you move towns or states.

Instead of avoiding everything like the plague, try cleansing places. For example I love the Melting Pot. Something about dipping little breads in melted cheese and fresh fruits in silky chocolate makes me happy. That's where my ex-husband proposed to me, where we had our first Valentine's Day dinner and an anniversary dinner. Obviously the Melting Pot brings up a lot of memories and ghosts that I don't want to have any more. Though, I don't want to take it out on the restaurant and I still want to be able to go there and enjoy myself.

In the act to cleanse the Melting Pot, I invited a bunch of friends for a girl's night out. We ate melted chocolate, drank wine and had a great time while cleansing the bad memories and replacing them with new, fun ones. Now when I think of the Melting Pot I remember the fun I had with my girlfriends instead of my ex-husband.

I recommend cleansing places for everyone. I think it's a good healing process when any relationship ends. One of the hardest things to get over is the fact that you spent most of your time with your ex. Every time you go out you're constantly reminded of things you did together. It makes it that much harder to get over someone. *You can't eat at this restaurant because that was your first date. Going to that movie theater is painful because you saw your favorite movie there together. Eating sushi breaks your heart because he used to make it for you.* Whatever the situation is, write them down. That will be your cleansing list. Then decide what you're going to do to record the new movie of your life and stop watching the re-runs.

It's fun to do and it's a reason to get people together. Have cleansing parties. It will help your mind, body and soul. Healing the past and moving on with your future. Pretty soon you'll go back to those favorite places you went to together and the ghosts will be gone completely. You won't even realize it. That's when you know you've healed your heart and moved on.

Healing the Loss of a Step-Child from Divorce

This topic doesn't seem to get much attention, but I think it's a very important one. This kind of loss is somewhat unique. What I'm referring to is when you are married to someone who already has children from a previous marriage. When you then divorce from that parent, you really have no rights to that child who was once your step-child. They were never maternally yours, yet you may have created a bond as a mother or father figure. When you separate from their maternal parent, especially if it wasn't on good terms, you may in fact lose contact with that child. It can be very devastating especially if you acted as a partial parent and spent a lot of time with them. It's a whole entirely different grieving process for that kind of loss.

There are all kinds of books out there for people dealing with divorce and separation and how to deal with their children, or even if a child dies. Yet there's nothing on the topic of dealing with the loss of a step-child. In a way it almost feels more like a death. To help raise a child for four years then, with no warning, have them ripped away from you with no opportunity to say goodbye. I had to figure out how to deal with the loss of my step-son myself, so this is why I'm adding this section-- to possibly help others who are dealing with the same issue.

During the four year relationship with my ex-husband I helped raised his son. I was in his life from about three to seven years old. I loved him and cared for him as if he was my own child. We had him every other weekend, holidays and half of the summer. I worked from home, so when he would stay with us during school breaks I cared for him during the day while my ex went to work. We had a special bond. On top of this unique situation he was also autistic. For me though this was never an issue. I grew up with a brother who has epilepsy so I knew how to interact with children who had special needs. My family also treated him as a grand-son. They loved him, he loved them, and it really was a great relationship despite the situation. He was also Hispanic and bi-lingual, my family Caucasian. I enjoyed trying to learn Spanish while watching Dora the Explorer with him.

When I discovered my ex was cheating on me, our happy family life all came to a halt. Everything happened so fast from moving out of our house, filing for divorce, to the final dissolution. It only takes 90 days in Florida to become divorced, if you are not disputing any terms. During all this, I was dealing with so many emotions and a broken heart that I didn't really have time to think about my step-son. I was busy trying to figure out where I was going to live and move on with my life. We were supposed to have him for a month in the summertime, yet we were divorced prior to that. I wanted to see him badly, but since he was only six and a half years old, so I would have to go through his father. It was too hard on me at the time. At this point I was not talking to my step-son's mother much because my ex didn't allow it. She used to live in Florida which made visitation easier since she had full custody, though a few months prior to our divorce she moved out to California and took my step-son with her.

As time passed and I was trying to move on with my life, the emotions from missing my step-son started to surface. Five months down the road my heart was breaking again, but this time for a different reason. I didn't know how to deal with losing him. I felt guilty, sad and I couldn't see or talk to him. I hadn't spoken to his mother at all. I didn't even know if she knew the whole story of what happened between his father and me. One day I was going through papers and discovered that I had my step-son's footprints from the hospital when he was born. That also reminded me that his birthday was right around the corner. I searched my inbox and found her email address. So I reached out to her and said I would send the papers to her and expressed my feelings for her son. She was very nice and, for the first time, we were able to speak truthfully about everything that had happened in my marriage.

She was very accommodating about if I wanted to see him again, yet they lived in California and I in Florida. I didn't have the money to travel out there. Instead, I bought him some presents for his 7th birthday. I wrote a card and expressed how much I loved him and missed him and that it wasn't his fault that I can't see him anymore. I also printed out pictures of us together and my cat Callie. He loved her a lot and his father told him she ran away and that's why she wasn't around anymore.

When the presents arrived she said that he loved all of it! His mother read him the card I wrote and tears muddled in his eyes. He was happy to see that Callie was ok and at home with me safe and sound. I added his mother on my Facebook as a friend so I can keep up with his doings and see photos. I send him a birthday present every year now and photos of Callie, so he can see her grow up. I know it's not as good as being there in person, though I do hope it helps him understand that I didn't want to leave him. I know it has helped me move on too, even though I still miss him greatly.

Moving On

It's now been about a year since I wrote the "Healing Wounds" chapter in my first book. It's brutally honest and I didn't sugar coat anything because I think it's so important to demonstrate what I was feeling at that particular time, like all the emotions I was dealing with from my divorce and the difficult relationship with my father. I literally came that morning from breakfast when I confronted him, got out my laptop and wrote the entire 10 or so pages. It's best from a writing point of view to get emotions down on paper when they're oozing out of your pores. I do what I call vomiting on the page. All my emotions and writing are pouring out of me. I don't care about grammar, spell check or formatting. Just as long as I get it on the page, then I clean it up later.

Now that I've had a year to grow, learn and develop from my big break through, I would love to say I have a wonderful relationship with my father. The reality is I don't. We've just barely gotten to the point where we talk. It's getting better, slowly as time goes by. But the thing is, I have changed, he has not. He can sense the change in me and that I'm not going to be bullied anymore or put up with bullshit. I'm not participating in the unhealthy, co-dependent relationship we used to have. I decided it wasn't good for me, so I ended it. He still tries to pull me back in, but I don't let it happen. If we are having a conversation and I see it going back to the old ways, I hang up the phone and end it.

Even though I accomplished what I set out to do when I left the car that day, publishing a book and now my second, I couldn't even bring myself to tell him that I had. At this point in my life I'm doing things to make myself proud, not anyone else, so I guess I just didn't really care. I eventually knew I would have to tell him or just let him find out for himself. One day he emailed me and asked what I had been up to lately. I had actually just pre-recorded an interview with Daytime TV. So I thought what a great way for him to discover all my accomplishments by showing him, not telling him. I responded to his email that he should tune into channel 11 and 11 AM on that upcoming Thursday. So he did and watched the show. He called me afterward and we had a nice conversation, however never did he once say, "I'm proud of you". Or that he was wrong about laughing in my face when I shared my dreams of becoming an author.

Now he's seen all my television interviews and the funny thing is, all he can do is criticize that I said this in one interview and not during another. I just laugh. Even my mother, she doesn't quite get it. When I called her excited about my first interview and the words out of her mouth were, "Why do they want to interview you?" Seriously! That hurt, like a knife in the heart. At least my mom will a few days later realize what she said and then try to make it better with a card or nice message. Either way, you can't always look for approval from outside sources, you can only get it within yourself. That's the best way I've discovered to make myself successful.

Even though it's only been a year, I feel like I have grown and matured 10 years fold. Now I can see the relationship I have with my father for what it is. Before, I always wished my father would change the way he treated me, like I was at his mercy; I was the victim. Now I have taken control and I know he will never change; I can only change myself and the way I handle the relationship. At this point I'm just trying to keep the peace between us. I'll do some real estate stuff, but only if I want to, not because I *have* to. I'm doing what I need to do for me first and then deciding what I have time left over for and where I want to put my energy. I do love my father and I always will. Sometimes I think we're both too similar and that's why we butt heads so much. The older he gets, the more stubborn he is. Now I know how to deal with it. I know it's not worth the fight. I smile, I nod and I proceed on with my life.

I did learn some valuable lessons from my father despite everything. He showed me how to live on barely anything and survive and that I can start my own business on a shoe-string budget. He instilled determination in me when he and other people said I would never accomplish my dreams, which made the desire burn inside me with a gas flame. I was going to succeed at all costs to prove everyone wrong. I definitely think everything happens for a reason and maybe if my course of life events wouldn't of been such I wouldn't be where I'm at today? Not really sure, though I cherish all my heart ache and suffering because I think it builds hungry people. Humans who hunger for victory are truly happy because they struggled so hard to get there. The others who have entitlement syndrome will never truly be content.

I know it's hard to stay positive when negative things are going on in your life. I used to be that person who hated the people who said, "Look at the silver lining". Sure how can I see that when I'm crying in my wine bottle after my second fiancé cheated on me and then I found out he was married six times prior with felony charges and a daughter he never paid child support for? Where's the silver lining in that?! Nevertheless, now I *am* that person who can see the light at the end of tunnel. It all makes sense now. So if you're in a rut and negative place in your life take a long hard look at yourself. What's wrong? What lessons are to be learned from this bad experience? Are you learning from them or repeating them over and over again?

From the Y Chromosome

1) Have you had any emotional wounds to heal before venturing out into the dating jungle?

Nathan – 28 – Single: *"I've had wounds to heal from jobs more than from dating. After college I did not get a job offer right away. Even though I excelled in my classes, it took over a year to get a job. Then when I finally did it wasn't a full time job. It really took a blow to my self-esteem. I had to restructure how I went about life. I did not spend my time dating in college, I instead studied and worked hard. So when I did venture out into the dating world, I would get stuck on one girl for almost a year without her showing any interest other than just being friends. I haven't seriously starting dating 'til a year ago. When I did start I was shy and wasn't connecting with anyone. I didn't have a posse full of guy fiends that would hook me up with girls, I had to do everything myself."*

Dan – 56 – in a LTR: **"***Women never break up with me, so I never really needed healing time. I've been dating online for six years now and I have never been dumped. Though, with my current live in girlfriend I really do love her, so if we broke up I might take six months off from dating. My longest relationship was four years long, though it didn't really seem like it because for the most part we only saw each other on the weekends. When I was 17 my first girlfriend started dating my best friend behind my back and then told me she liked him more than me, which hurt. That's really the only emotional wounds I've have yet I was in high school so it doesn't really count."*

Chris – 41 – Divorced: *"I think it's really important, though how do you know when you've healed yourself? Hopefully you have good friends to help you out. With my ex she was trying to put the blame on me. I tried to keep my friends out of it in the beginning. But she kept turning the* *tables, making me think what did I do wrong, what's wrong with me? So I started talking to my friends about our situation and they helped me realize I tried as hard as I could, but she was moving on with her life and I needed to as well. I think you know once you've healed yourself from the past once you stop talking about your ex on dates with other people. When you can recognize the difference between other women and your ex, it's a sign your over them."*

Jerry – 60 – in a LTR: *"Absolutely, it's very important to heal yourself after a relationship. Plus you don't want to submit a woman into a transiently relationship."*

2) How long do you wait from one break up before venturing onto finding the next?

Chris – 41 – Divorced: *"I went on dating sites rights away to see who was out there. It did this because it's going to take a while to find someone. But you need to be honest about your situation. We didn't have kids so she moved out right away and we filed for divorce. It took a year for the finalization. I started dating before the divorce was official, however we never had contact during that separation period."*

Jerry – 60 – in a LTR: *"When I got divorced it was a friendly one because we wanted to continue to be good parents to our children. We had just grown differently in our relationship. We tried counseling and during that period we both realized there was nothing left to save. It took a year to sell our house because of the bad real estate market, so we were separated but continued to live in the house together. We both started dating before we sold the house, but I was honest and would tell women we were living together. Some it bothered others it didn't. At first when I started to date again I thought I was fine because there were not many hurt feelings within my divorce. My ex and I never bad mouthed one another because of our two daughters. Subsequently I realized I was coming off as desperate. I was like a horse coming out of the gate at full speed. I went on ten dates in the first month. So I decided to take six months off to get back to myself. My personal rule is if it's been less than* *a year from your divorce being finalized, you will end up in a transiently relationship with someone, not a long term relationship."*

OVERVIEW: Rule #1

- Are you ready to date or do you need to take some time off from life first?
- Heal ALL wounds before you love another; it doesn't matter if they came from a past divorce, an old romance, or even a traumatic childhood.
- You're damaged goods & won't be able to see things clearly going into the dating jungle until you heal yourself.
- Get therapy if you need to & take all the time you need.
- Use burning therapy and cleansing places to help you.
- You can't change other people, you can only change yourself.

RULE #2
FIND THE RIGHT WEBSITE FOR YOU

Once you have healed your wounds and are ready to navigate the internet dating jungle, you need to first decide which dating website will be the best for you. There are all kinds of sites out there today. Depending upon your personality, choosing the right site can make a big difference in whom you discover. You may need to test out multiple sites, though I recommend trying out one site at a time. It's embarrassing to not remember who you met where.

In this chapter I will review the most popular and some of the unusual dating sites on the internet. I have been on quite a few and have real world experience meeting men from them. I'll let you know the functionality, how much they cost (at the time when I signed up), and what types of people are on them. I'll also tip you in on the sites that are 100 percent free and the ones who claim to be, but in reality are not.

Internet Dating Terminology

Before I get into the review of the different dating sites, I first want to go over dating terminology. This is important especially if you are not used to meeting people online. There's an entire vocabulary that is used out in the internet dating jungle. If you do not know what these acronyms mean, you could get yourself in trouble. Here's a breakdown of the most popular dating terms I've come across:

Puma – A woman in her 30's dating a younger man

Cougar – A woman in her 40's dating a younger man

Lioness – A woman in her 50's dating a younger man

Sugar Daddy – Generally an older, wealthy man dating a younger woman

Sugar Baby – A younger woman dating an older, wealthy man

Sugar Momma – An older, wealthy woman dating a younger man

Seeking Arrangement – Someone looking for a non-traditional relationship where there is no commitment involved and services are exchanged for elaborate gifts

SWF – Single White Female

SWM – Single White Male

WSW – Woman Seeking Women

MSM – Man Seeking Men

MSW – Man Seeking Women

WSM – Woman Seeking Men

LTR – Long Term Relationship

BBW – Big Beautiful Woman

NSA – No Strings Attached

MWF – Man with Female (used when couples are seeking other couples)

MWM – Man with Man

HWP – Height Weight Proportionate

D&D – Drugs & Disease Free

SBF – Single Black Female

SBM – Single Black Male

SUB – Submissive

DOM – Dominant/ Dominatrix

FWB – Friends with Benefits (just sex, no commitment)

W4M -Woman for Men

M4W – Men for Women

SD – Sugar Daddy

SB – Sugar Baby

The Lifestyle – usually refers to swingers

Swinger - A person who engages in consensual sex with people or couples outside of their core relationship

TS – Transsexual

TG – Transgender

M4T – Man for Transvestite

T4M – Transvestite for Man

Sissy – A male transvestite that wants to be treated like a female slut and dominated

CD – Cross Dresser

Gurl – A man wanting to be a woman

S&M - Sadist / Masochist or Slave/ Master: The sadist inflicts pain and asserts control over the masochist

Demisexual - A person who does not experience sexual attraction unless they form a strong emotional connection with someone. They do not have primary sexual instincts.

Review of Plenty of Fish POF.com

This is a very popular dating website. They claim to have more dates, more relationships and more visits than any other site. This partially could be true because it's one of the rare sites that is 100 percent free. Other sites claim to be free, such as Zoosk, yet after you create a profile that's it. You can't do anything else. To me that's not free. Instead, it's just a bait and switch, which is really irritating.

As of right now (7/18/2012 at 2:51 p.m. EST), Plenty of Fish claims to have 386,846 users online. That's quite substantial. You can pay to be a gold member and unlock more features, yet the free version is enough to be able to create a profile, upload pictures and communicate with users. I really don't see a point in paying for it.

Another good aspect of this site, other than it being 100 percent free, is the functionality. They must make enough from all the advertising to pay someone to program the software because it functions well. The ads across the top are annoying, yet if you can get past that, it's fine. This site also has the best instant message that I have seen so far other than OkCupid. It actually works when you send a message. You can chat pretty easily online with someone and with multiple people at once. The only thing I wish they would improve is to have an alert noise when you receive a message. If you minimize the IM window and go back to check your e-mail, you aren't aware if the person responds.

The blocking feature works well and is easy to use. If you get a nasty message from someone, right in the e-mail at the bottom is the option to block someone. I like that. It's easy to see new messages that you have since they are in grey. Once you read it, that line goes white. You can also change your settings to filter out who can e-mail you which is handy. For example, I don't want anyone e-mailing me without a photo. I have mine on there; they know what I look like so I want to know what users e-mailing me look like.

Also included in the free portion of the site are features so you can see who has viewed your profile, add favorite profiles and fill out the chemistry questionnaire. I have not completed the chemistry questionnaire portion of the site. I don't really believe in a computer actually being able to tell you if you're compatible with someone. Chemistry is something you can only evaluate in person, not by answering questions on a computer.

POF also has a free mobile app which I have used on the iPhone. It's fairly user friendly. The only bugs I have noticed is if I'm out and about and type a lengthy response, half the time it times out and says it cannot connect to the servers and then logs me out. That is annoying because now I have lost my entire e-mail. If I log back in, it's completely erased and I have to write it all over again. Most the time I don't even bother, so some guys might get the crappy end of the deal here. Not because I didn't want to respond, but the app lost connection and I don't have time to retype e-mails five times.

Other times I have responded to multiple e-mails and then I don't get a response. Once I log into the website on my laptop, I look and it says the message was never sent, which is definitely annoying. I got into the habit of reading the e-mails on my iPhone then responding when I had the proper time and internet connection to do so. If you do read your e-mails on the app, it will reflect that in the website when you log in.

The only downfall to this site being free is that it attracts anyone and everyone. With paid sites you can usually weed out the people who are just joking around and not serious about finding a relationship. I do consider Plenty of Fish the Wal-Mart of dating sites. Walk into a Wal-Mart and those are the guys and girls that are on this dating site. Why? Because it's free!

I admit I go to Wal-Mart because I, too, want to save money on my groceries. Low prices attract ALL kinds of people. You're going to have your white trash, the mom with eight kids, the single parent, the college partier, the divorcee and everything in-between. Just like at Ross, there are some great discount deals on Ralph Lauren shirts, but you have to carefully weed through all the junk to find them. I'm all about finding a diamond in the rough, so I guess I don't mind this challenge. If you want your perfect match handed to you on a platter, POF probably isn't the site for you. It takes a lot of time to filter out through all the e-mails to find a decent person. Trust me; they are out there, but you need to be prepared for what else you'll encounter.

I've received e-mails from guys looking for a booty call and saying nasty things to kids just joking around. It's all a numbers game. Especially if you're reasonably attractive girl or guy, you're going to get tons of emails. It's best to establish a strategy. I only e-mail back to about 25 percent of the messages I receive. There's no way I could respond to everyone even if I wanted to. I set up a filter, which included the top five things I'm looking for in a mate. If the profile doesn't match, next! I'll decide within two minutes if I'm going to respond or not, quick and to the point. (I'll go over this online weeding out process in a future chapter.)

I went on a few dates from this site. I did eventually have two short term relationships. One was good the other one not so much. The first relationship I had since my divorce was actually with a man I met on POF. I think it was also one of the healthiest ones I've had in a long time. He was very nice, a little older than me, and we got along great. But sometimes after a month or so you realize it's not the right person for you to spend the rest of your life with. We had some differences in opinions and lifestyles, so we parted ways and are still good friends.

In conclusion, I would give Plenty of Fish 7 out of 10 stars. The overall site functions very well, though the layout and graphics are not the best. At least they have an app, but it could use some adjusting. As for the people on there? Well, like I said, it's definitely an online Wal-Mart. Take from it what you can. Remember, it's free! Don't get upset by weirdoes, losers and others that are on there to serve as a nuisance. Block them and move on, and with a little patience, eventually you'll come across your pearl in the ocean.

Plenty of Fish Hook-A-Fish Event Review

POF.com has local events to get singles out from behind their laptops to meet in the flesh. I like the concept, so I thought I would check one out to review for my book and blogs. My roommate went with me who is divorced and 50 years old. This event was held at a bar in a hotel on the water in Tarpon Springs, Florida. We signed in, got a name tag and the place was packed, good sign. Unfortunately, I was the youngest person there by oh 20 years, bad sign. There was no age limit on the event and I don't know if it's the venue or the area that pulls a much older crowd, yet it definitely wasn't my cup of tea.

Everyone seemed to be having a good time, which is great. However, I'm 35 so my demographic was not at that event. Since I knew I wasn't looking for a boyfriend in their 60's, I decided to have one drink and call it a night. I wanted to make sure my roommate had a ride home, so as I finished my wine waiting for her friends to show up, I had various offers from men. One of which was to leave the event and go eat some of his homemade chili. I politely declined. Finally her friends came and I left. As I was in the parking lot heading to my car, a man that could have been my grandpa asked me why I was leaving so soon. Hmmm how do I nicely reply, "I don't want to date anyone who is collecting social security?"

The next day my roommate said she had a great time. Nonetheless, I don't think I will attend another one of POF's events. It wasn't the caliber of men I am interested in. The only very few younger ones more or less looked like the guys I would block from the website. My conclusion is that if you're 50 or older it may be fun. Or if it was held in a different venue then younger people will show up? I'm not sure, though I think I'll just stick to meeting the men online.

Review of Match.com

I've personally been off and on Match a few times. I ventured on there when I moved out to California after college to meet new people. I dated two guys I met online. Each relationship lasted a few months and nothing wonderful came from it, but nothing awful either. The last time I went onto Match was about a year after my divorce while I was working at a real estate law firm. This time I was on Match it was about $35 for a one month subscription and a free seven day trial. I did the free trial because I didn't want to pay. I had one date from it and it was a date from hell. Literally, he was one of the biggest assholes I've meet online. I hadn't dated in months and this guy wasn't giving me any good reasons to venture back out into the dating jungle.

The few guys I met this last time on Match all seemed very desperate. If I didn't call or text back ASAP they would freak out. If a first date didn't turn into a marriage proposal at the end of the night, the guy would freak out.

I chatted with one guy who was almost 10 years older than me for maybe three or four days before he asked me out. He invited me to dinner at a place close to where we both lived. I agreed even though he was at the top of my age range. I was surprised he was asking me out because when I looked at his profile I didn't think we had much in common. He seemed uptight, but he assured me he was very easy going; I accepted his invitation and we met the next night. I was dressed in very nice, classy but feminine attire: a knee length, flowy skirt, nice blouse, a little sweater, and heels. He had on a button down and khakis. As he opened his mouth everything that came out just reinforced the fact that we *really* didn't see eye-to-eye on anything. He was looking for some June Cleaver, Bible Beater, and house wife when I specifically had non-religious, career-woman checked on my profile. Though me being an adult, I chose to suffer through my meal, drink two glasses of wine to listen to his crap and still maintain a smile on my face until dinner was over. Thank goodness that part came quickly. He walked me to my car and said that uncomfortable departure sentence as he gave me a hug, "Let's get together soon."

I nodded "sure" but my mind was screaming *"no way in hell will I ever talk to you again!"* I chalked it up to a bad date; I would never see or hear from again. Instead, to my surprise, he texted me the next day while I was at work. I deleted the text unfortunately, but it went a little something like this: *"I am so disappointed in last night. You looked nothing like your photos, we had nothing in common and it was a big waste of my time. I can't believe I spent money on you."*

WOW, are you kidding me? Most guys I've gone out with from the internet say I look better in person than my photos. How rude! I knew we had nothing in common before we went out, but apparently he didn't *read* my profile. He just looked at my photos, which I always keep current. So I have no idea what image he had in his head of me prior, but I can tell you I already knew I wasn't going to fit into his "Stepford Wife" mold. Why did I even go out with him in the first place? Who knows; I'm an optimistic person to the bitter end and that time it definitely bit me in the ass.

I chose to be the bigger person once again with this douche bag and didn't respond to his text message. I just deleted it. Now I wish I would have saved it to put in my book because he was truly awful and rude. He is the reason why I created the dating rule about initial short meet-n-greets, which I'll go into more detail later in the book.

I had a few other bad dates from Match.com, but that one took the cake. Nonetheless, I just brushed myself off and jumped back on the horse again. As for the functionality of the site goes, I'm not that impressed. It's a paid site and they must be making tons of money. I have a few girlfriends who paid the $150 for a year subscription. I only did a month because I didn't want to be on there for an entire year. I knew I would get tired of it by then. For a paid site it should work way better than it does.

The chat doesn't work much at all. When you go log in and check emails, it doesn't un-highlight it, so when I go back it's hard to find out who I replied to and/or which emails I've read. POF's site functions way better and it's totally free. Where exactly is Match putting its funds? Towards expensive TV commercials, perhaps? They should re-invest it back into their computer programmers.

My experience was that the same guys that are on POF are also on Match, so why pay to talk with the same people? Go over to POF and get it for free. One guy I dated a few times was on both and he could never remember which site he met me on. It was funny because he would always look perplexed when we spoke about it. He asked me one day, "Why do you still have your profile up on POF?" I responded that we met on Match. You could see the gerbils and small wheels turning inside his head as he couldn't tell his dating sites apart.

Another huge downfall with Match is that they do not have a mobile app. It's annoying when you're out and about and want to check your email from your smart phone and you have to go to the full website to login. You can't read anything and it's all micro sized. Then people try to IM you while you're logged in for a few seconds. Not like it works anyway, but they think you're online when really you're only on your mobile phone; you couldn't even try to utilize the chat feature even if you wanted to.

I'm giving Match.com 5 out of 10 stars. The site functionality stinks, there's no mobile app, the stir events are no fun (see below), and you have to pay for it.. The only reason I'm even giving it 5 stars is because after interviewing the men and speaking to many more, from the male prospective they like Match better. The men say there is a higher caliber of women on there and the 2 out of 4 I interviewed both met their current relationship on that site.

Review of Stir Events for Match.com

Match.com now has events for members called Stir. You may have seen them advertised on TV. It sounds like a fun idea, a bar full of people who you know for sure are single. No second guessing or looking for the tan line of the wedding ring on the finger. Everyone should be open and ready to mingle! My girlfriend and I were both on Match, saw this event and decided to check it out.

This event was held in Channelside area of Tampa at a posh bar. We decided to have appetizers and a drink across the street prior to venturing over. Arriving about 30-45 minutes after it started, it was still fairly sparse. As we did a quick lap around, it became apparent that most of these men are on Match for a reason. We grabbed a beer, stood in the center and felt eyes burning holes all over my body. It was an adult version of a bad high school prom scene. Most people join a dating website because they are busy in their life and are sick of the bar scenes. Other people join dating sites because they have no social skills to actually approach women. This obviously seemed to be the latter going on at this event. Take a bunch of guys that don't know how to approach a woman out from behind their computers, throw them in a bar and guess what, they still don't know how to approach a woman!

We stood there beer in hand and all the men slowly walked around us like lions circling their prey wondering which one was going to pounce on the fresh meat first. Unfortunately none of them seemed to have the skill set to do so. So we stood there all eyes staring at us feeling completely awkward. As the night got later, more people did arrive. Most of the guys were still not anyone I was interested in. There were only two that seemed like a possibility the entire night.You could tell they had it all going on. Good looking, charismatic, not really even dressed up, yet had this magnetic pull to them. I was actually intrigued in possibly getting to know one of them, but after observing them, I realized every other woman in the place wanted to get to know them too. My girlfriend had been chatting with a guy from Match.com prior to the event. They had a date scheduled for the following day. When she brought up his profile on her phone, I recognized him right away. He had contacted me on two different sites before. I never responded because he had the creep factor just from his photos. She told him earlier that day she was going to the Stir event, I figured that was a bad idea. It was. He showed up about 15 minutes after our conversation and stood in the corner behind us just staring at her. It was bluntly obvious he recognized her because he followed us wherever we went, yet wouldn't approach her, just stood a few feet away at all times. We eventually spoke to a few guys at the event and once we did, he made his move, if you call it that. He swooped over out of nowhere. Then stuck his face right into hers as if he was going in for a kiss, but pulled back without missing a step and disappeared into the crowd. After that, we decided to chalk the night up to one big disappointment. The next day my girlfriend canceled her date with the stalker. He responded with, "Did you attend the Stir event last night?" She decided not to respond to that email.

My opinion of the Stir event from Match.com is: if it's free, sure why not? There will be different kinds of people at different events. Some events are pricey though. I myself wouldn't pay to attend one of these. Some of my other friends attended various Stir events and had similar experiences.

Review of eHarmony.com

What cracks me up about the site is their "patented matching technology." Their technology consists of a bunch of questions that you fill in about yourself, like a bubble scantron vote ballot. Its accuracy is just about as good as how fast Florida counts votes. Filling in dots about yourself and then having a computer match you with a guy or girl who fills in the same type of answers doesn't mean you have *chemistry*. That is only something two people can discover in person, one on one. No online computer software can mimic that.

I've had a couple of friends, men and women, take the lengthy time to fill out their entire questionnaire, to only at the bitter end be rejected by the system. Seriously, eHarmony said they did not have *anyone* in their system to match them up with. WOW, what a slap in the face! Imagine that you're already apprehensive about entering the dating jungle, then their robot, who doesn't know squat other than matching bubbles, tells you, *"Hey man, might as well give up and go jump off a chair because no woman wants to meet you."*

The president claims that they have 20 million users within their system. There are absolutely no matches at all from those 20 million people? I found that hard to believe and so does one of the founders of OkCupid, Christian Rudder, who wrote a little article I found interesting. Now, he obviously has a biased opinion trying to bash the competition, yet his article makes sense. This is not the entire article, but it is the meat of the point. (If you want to read the entire article you can visit my blog: tampadatingjungle.wordpress.com)

The "20 Million Members" Paradox of eHarmony

eHarmony claims over 20 million members on their homepage, and their CEO, Greg Waldorf, reiterates that number regularly in interviews. If your goal is to find someone special, 20 million people is a lot of options—roughly a quarter of all singles in the U.S. This sounds awesome until you realize that most of these people can't reply, because only paying customers are allowed to message.

So let's now ask the real question: of these 20 million people eHarmony claims you can flirt with, how many are actually able to flirt back? They closely guard their number of paid subscribers, with good reason. Nonetheless, we are able to deduce their base from known information. We'll give eHarmony the highest subscribership possible with a little bit a math of their revenue divided by the month memberships fees to comes a conclusion that only 1/30th of the "20 million users" they advertise is someone you can actually talk to. That's the paradox: the more they pump up their membership totals to convince you to sign up, the worse they look.

Basically what he's saying in his article is that most of the "users" eHarmony claims to have are dead accounts. If you're frustrated that you are not getting many matches on their site, it could be the fact that there are not as many people actively using their account. The short time I was on eHarmony and went on a few dates with my matches, none of them ended up being anyone I was interested in dating. I think my mom could have done a better job setting me up than this site. The website will not show you the photo of the person you're a supposedly match for until everything else matches at the very end. I don't think you should only judge a person on their looks, but attraction is still a big piece of the pie.

I give eHarmony 1 out of 10 stars. You can pay the hefty fee of $59.95 per month to interact with dead accounts, but I still think testing out a free site first is the way to go. Though, I've noticed while conducting interviews with men about online dating experiences that they seem to have different opinions. Men seem to prefer paid sites over the free ones because they say the quality of women are better on those. From my point of view, it's the same people on paid sites that are on free ones.

Review of OkCupid.com

I heard many good and bad things about this site from various people prior to actually joining it myself. I finally did and I'm glad. This is another site that is 100 percent for free. There are no tricks or games. You can create a profile, upload pictures and interact with people . The site is very user friendly and the look and feel is more modern versus POF. After using OkCupid, POF seems like a 90's version of OkCupid's sleek, modern design.

Their Instant Message chat feature works unlike Match.com. I wish the IM feature had a little noise or bell to it when someone sends you a message, which would be helpful. If you like to multi-task on your computer and someone sends you an IM on OkCupid, you have no idea until you pull up that internet window again and look. It was the same problem with all the other dating sites that had the IM feature, but it does function so that's a plus.

OkCupid also has a free mobile app that is easy to use. The messages seem to always go through and I didn't have the problem like I did with POF app where I would write a message and then it never actually sent. The only thing I did notice, which is also a problem with the POF mobile app, is when I get new messages it doesn't populate them to the top. So my phone will buzz and notify me of a new message, and when I scroll down I cannot tell who the message was from. If I click on the old message the new message will show up, yet I couldn't tell before I opened that string it was that person who sent the message. When you're carrying on a few conversations at once, it makes it difficult. Using the website it definitely easier in that regard.

When you log in with the mobile app, though, it will say that you are online. I don't like that aspect because really I'm not online, I'm mobile. If I want to check my emails on my iPhone while I'm walking on the treadmill, I don't necessarily want everyone to think I'm online. Plus, more people usually email you when your status says online. Then it makes it harder to read and respond to the emails I wanted to. Sometime I'll check my email at a stop light. Then when I close the app when I start driving it still says I'm online. It looks like I'm on the site all day long when in reality I'm not.

They also have a section where you can answer questions about yourself. An example would be: "Would you have sex on a first date?" Yes or No? Then they will ask you to rank how important that question topic is to you. The more questions you answer the better because it will then rate your answers with other users. It calculates a percentage that you are a Match, Friend or Enemy with that person. It's obviously not perfect, but it's kind of cool to see that and how other people answer the same questions. The personality section is interpreted based on your answers to the questions and how your personality may lean towards a more spiritual, less progressive, intellectual and so on.

While you're on the website, little notices pop up in the bottom to tell you who has visited your profile and/or sent you a message. Every time you check out someone's profile, they will obviously do the same to that person. You can surf profiles anonymously if you want to, but you have to turn on that feature first. When you're searching profiles it also tells you how often a user receives emails and how often they reply to emails. I'm not really sure I like that feature. It's like saying he or she isn't popular; they have received no emails this week. Or this girl barely responds to emails, so no point in emailing her. Maybe they are not interested in the emails they receive? I wonder how they figure that out. Do they rate it based on how often you are logged onto their site and emails you hit reply to? What if you didn't log onto the site for a week and you were on vacation so you didn't reply to any emails?

I met three men from OkCupid and chatted with multiple guys. As always, there were a few bad apples. I noticed a few of the same guys from POF were also on OkCupid. Though, surprisingly there were a lot I had not seen on any other dating sites which is why testing out one site at a time is the best method. If you see a person on multiple sites you can come off as serial dater. Nobody wants to go out with a serial dater (one who engages in the process of systematically dating an obscene amount people in short span of time; this term can be considered a politically correct alternative to the word "player," both with and without a negative connotation).

The dates I went on with the men on OkCupid were much better versus the ones from Match.com. Actually dates from POF and OkCupid were far better than Match.com. Though, I also was utilizing more of my "weeding out" technique which greatly helps. Yes, I had some nasty emails and weirdoes, but I didn't engage in endless emails with them. If they became annoying or rude I just blocked them. If you can't behave online, then I definitely don't want to meet you in person.

I give OkCupid 9 out of 10 stars. The site functions great, the mobile app works well, it's free, and I found the quality of dates higher on this site versus the other ones.

<u>Review of Sugardaddie.com</u>

This is a controversial website, hence the name Sugar Daddie. I've tested it out a few times. I initially joined this site because I was tired of the guys from POF and other sites that didn't have a job or a car or a driver's license. I wanted a guy who was established, knew what they wanted and how to get it. I have a lot of drive and ambition and I was looking for the same in a partner.

Their site claims that it is the classy place to meet people online, the finest people on internet dating: where the classy, attractive and affluent meet. Everyone has to pay for the site. Some sites like these make the men pay and it's free for women. Here everyone pays $20 a month. You can pay for a year and get a discount or you can just go month to month. What I do like about this site is that when you pay for a month, they do not automatically renew your membership. You pay for the month, that's what you get, and at the end it expires. Your profile will still be there, yet you will not be able to read any of the emails that you receive.

The site's overall functionality isn't bad, though their IM feature hardly works at all. Half the time if someone tries to IM, you can get the little window to open up. If you enter certain characters in the window it will cut of all the words after that. Such as if you sent a sentence like: "I've lived in FL for 10 years, but I moved here from Nebraska and lived in CA for 1 year." The only part that would go through is "I've lived in FL for 10 years."

My experience from this site was pretty plain and simple. Old, nasty rich guys are looking for young, hot chicks. Many of the men on this site are married, though they don't seem to care and are willing to pay for the company of a beautiful woman. I received so many off the wall offers from this site it could really be a book of its own. I did not come across any men that were actually looking for a long term relationship besides one: an older gentleman who claimed he would pay off all my credit cards and student loans if I married him. Interesting proposition, yet nothing in life comes for free. I would have definitely been "paying" my debt off for the rest of my life.

Men on this site do not have any apprehension to ask for exactly what they want. Fetishes are fairly prominent on here as well. One man's fetish was to be treated like a dog. He offered me money to meet him at a hotel room, tie him up in a dog cage, feed him dog food and call him Fido. This was awhile back so I do not recall the amount of money he offered, but I declined anyway. I don't think I have it in me to treat someone like a dog. Just not in my nature. I've been offered $1,000 to spend a lavish weekend with someone. These men know what they want and are not afraid to pay for it.

Another guy wanted me to kick him in the balls as hard as I could. He said he was going to hold a $20 bill in his mouth and he wanted me to kick him so hard until he dropped it out of his mouth! Needless to say I didn't do that either. There are a lot of fetishes out there which brings me to wonder *why* people have certain fetishes, such as the foot fetish, the dog fetish, the kick me so hard in the balls my face turns purple fetish. It must be from a traumatic childhood. I personally have no fetishes. I'm pretty normal and enjoy normal things. Although all these fetishes intrigue me, they do not interest me enough to engage in them with anyone.

I did meet one man in person from Sugardaddie.com We went on a few dates and, I believe it was the third one, when we were back at my place making out and I could just tell he was a little kinky just by the way he held my hands down with super mutant strength; he was very thin and lanky. When I asked him if he was into odd sexual stuff his response was, "Isn't it hot when you think back into the caveman days when a man would club a woman over the head and drag her back to his cave and have his way with her?"

Ummmm no! It's not hot. I think in modern day times that is considered rape?! I totally freaked out after that and kicked him out of my place. He kept reassuring me he wasn't a weirdo or rapist and was just into S&M stuff. Well I don't know anything about bondage, or whips-n-chains. I grew up in the Midwest, not saying we are all normal, but I have never heard of any of this strange sexual stuff until I moved to Florida back in 2002.

Of course my curiosity got the better of me and I started doing research on bondage. Apparently there is a large community of people all into this kind of stuff; pain, pleasure, dog food—you name it, someone's into it. I thought I would give this guy the benefit of the doubt and be his friend; who am I judge what turns someone on? I think I was interested in finding out why he was into these kinds of things. Plus I can be friends with pretty much anyone.

One day we were going out to dinner together as friends, and I was over at his place while he was getting ready. When he was in the shower he told me not to go in his closet. Well of course, what do I do? I go into his closet. OMG. I had no idea how much he was seriously into this bondage stuff. His walk in closet was full of all the normal guy things shirts, pants and shoes. Then, as I turned to look closer, from floor to ceiling on the left were ball gags, whips, dildos, anal probes and other sex toys I don't even know what the names of. You think that would be the freaky part, but what was more odd was that they were all neatly organized in plastic zip lock baggies.

This guy is "50 Shades of Grey," the real deal minus being a billionaire. I personally have not read the "50 Shades of Grey" series, I'm waiting for the movie. All of my girlfriends have, though, and they think it's all glamorous and sexy. I keep telling them if they want to experience it in real life I can hook them up with my friend. No one ever takes me up on my offer...

I give Sugardaddie.com 6 out of 10 stars. I like the fact they don't keep charging you month after month, thought the IM sucks. When signing up for this site you just need to know what you are getting yourself into.

Review of SugarDaddyForMe.com

This site is like a low class version of the original SugarDaddie.com. They also charge for this site to talk and interact with other users. It's still the same concept as the other SD site: older guys looking for younger women and are willing to provide elaborate gifts. I had the same offers on here as I did the other Sugar Daddie site.

SugarDaddyForMe.com has a free, three day teaser membership, and then you have to pay. You have to enter your credit card for the free trial as well. If you don't cancel within 24 hours before the last day you will be charged. The first time I tried it I canceled in 48 hours and I was good. The second time I did not cancel and I was charged for a month's membership. So I figured what the hell, I'll try it out for a month. I did and then I wanted to cancel. This is when it got ugly.

They have nowhere on their site to actually cancel a membership. You have to send an email, which is completely absurd. I followed their instructions and sent an email to cancel. Of course, it charged me the next month which really ticked me off. There's no phone number on their site to call and speak to a human being. I sent dozens of emails to the address listed to cancel. I never *received* a reply. Instead of being charged a third month, I had to call my bank and have them put a stop on it and have them contact the company about the second month's charge. Two weeks later, the company *finally* responded and tried to offer me a discount. Seriously?! I don't want a discount; I want your stupid company to STOP charging my account!

I give SugarDaddyForMe.com 1 out of 10 stars. It was a nightmare to deal with and a crappy site overall. If you want to do a Sugar Daddy site, stick with SugarDaddie.com. At least they will not rip you off!

Review of Zoosk.com

Zoosk.com claims to be a free dating site, it even pulls up as a free dating site in Google, yet it's not free. Yes, you can create a profile for free and upload your photos for free, but you cannot email anyone or respond for free. You have to buy coins in order to interact with people. It really irritated me after I spent the time to create the profile, only to discover it was not 100 percent free. To me it was a bait and switch. I then didn't *want* to pay because I felt lied to. I did receive emails from users, but I never interacted with any of them. It was a pain in the butt to take my profile off from the site as well. I think I may still even have a profile floating out there somewhere. This is where dating sites such as eHarmony inflate their numbers. I have basically a dead profile on their site, but I'm sure they count me as a user.

I give Zoosk 1 out of 10 stars. If your site isn't free, don't advertise it as being free.

Review of Craigslist.org

You can buy and sell anything on Craigslist, everything from prostitutes to couches, so it's crazy to think you could find someone to fall in love with there, too. If you venture onto Craigslist land, just be aware that there are all kinds of people and things on it: lots of naked photos, penis photos, and everything else you could imagine. It is free, no misconception there, just look and post your ad in the right section. This is where the dating terminology section comes in handy.

I posted an ad once on Craigslist. I was in-between relationships before my marriage and just wanted someone to go out to dinner and see a movie with. I posted an ad on a Friday around 4 p.m. I uploaded a photo and within 20 minutes, I had 50 or so email replies. About an hour later I took it down because my inbox was flooded. I weeded it down to a few prospective guys, and then finally one, who I did meet out for dinner and a movie. He was young, cute, and smart. We actually ended up dating for three months after the fact. I was pleasantly surprised since it was my first experience with a personal ad on Craigslist.

I met another couple who met on Craigslist and are engaged. They laugh as well when they tell the story of how they met. It just shows you can meet decent people anywhere. Just be careful as you would with any dating website. Make sure you are surfing the right section of craigslist, especially since there are lots of scams which could be men from India posing as beautiful women who are just trying to get a cashier's check. Obviously, never give out bank account information or any other personal stuff.

"Choosing safer sex for you and your partner greatly reduces the risk of contracting STDs including HIV." They actually have this posted on their warning and disclaimer portion of the personal ad section. I'm not sure if I should laugh or be disturbed. They also state that Craigslist has implemented the PICS system to assist with content filtering. Well I, of course, had to see for myself and NO their PICS system does not work. I was appalled by the photos I saw. I can't even start to describe what they were of. The messed up thing is that it's a public website and even though you have to click to state that you are 18 or older, which is only saving their butts from prosecution, any child out there could see this. I think my eyeballs are scorned for life.

I give Craigslist 1 out of 10 stars. It is free, yet be careful where you go and what you click on. Since the site is not very closely monitored everything gets on there. You might be conversing with a transgender prostitute, which is fine if that's what you're looking for. At least the other free sites like OkCupid and POF do filter stuff out like naked photos and most scammers. Craigslist does not; it's definitely buyer-beware.

From the Y Chromosome

1) Which dating website did you have the best results on and why?

Nathan – 28 – Single: *"OkCupid.com because I have been on this site longer. It's also easier to message women on here, they respond more often. It seems I have more stuff in common with women on this site. The percentage match of friend or enemy is interesting, yet I don't base my entire opinion of them from it. I will usually read a woman's profile first, but sometimes I have emailed without reading it and only based on their photos."*

Dan – 56 – in a LTR: *"Match.com and POF.com. There are more normal women on Match yet POF has weekly meet-up parties and is free. I've had good luck on both of those sites."*

Chris – 41 – Divorced: *"I honestly don't like any of them. I went on a few dates from Match.com. I like OkCupid because of the questions you can answer to see how much you have in common and it's free."*

Jerry – 60 - in a LTR: *"Match.com because there's always a new supply of women on there. Plus they have six months guarantee. If you don't meet anyone within six months they give you another six months free. Jdate.com was a good site as well since I'm Jewish; however there are lots of non-Jewish women on there. I believe it's because Jewish men treat their women well. It didn't bother me though because I don't really hold religion as a super important aspect in my life. I'm more spiritual. Jewish was bonus points but not a deal breaker."*

2) Which website had the worst results and why?

Nathan – 28 – Single: *"Singlesnet.com was the first dating site I ever* *used. You were limited for what you could put on profile. The women on there were trashy, though it could be the area that I was living searching in too. That was about 4 – 5 years ago. It was $90 for the year. I was only on it for 7-8 months. I met up with only one girl and she was crazy also had a kid. Was on Christine Singles but never met anyone from that site. Better quality women are on Match.com and EHarmony.com. Though with EHarmony it's about $300 for the year and you can't search profiles yourself, they send you matches. Basically Match and EHarmony have the high class/ popular girls, whereas OkCupid contains goth girls and biker chicks."*

Dan – 56 – in a LTR: *"Yahoo singles it was a long time ago but I just remember that site stunk."*

Chris – 41 – Divorced: *"POF has lots of fake profiles. Women will have attractive photos and say they're 38 years old with kids, then after a few emails I find out they're 65 instead. I've also had hookers email me from that site. I do not like EHarmony just because they don't allow same sexes to email one another. I'm straight, yet I don't want to support a company that has those kinds of beliefs."*

Jerry – 60 – in a LTR: *"I was on EHarmony when it first came out, I did the 30 days free trail. They would match you up with someone then you had to send three questions to the other person and then they responded with three questions and you each had to do that three times. At the end you would finally get a photo of the other person. By that time it took so long, my 30 days was up and I couldn't see the picture. It wasted so much time I didn't even want to pay for it to see who the women were. I was also on fitness-singles.com though there's not a plentiful of new people that join there.*

3) What's your worst online dating experience?

Nathan – 28 – Single: *"I had to block girl that was sending tons of* emails from OKCupid. She was fat and ugly and didn't get the hint I wasn't into her. Singlesnet.com was full of scammers with generic profiles. They will send messages that they're vacationing in West Africa and lost credit card and need money to get home. Other sites will weed out scammers better."

Dan – 56 – in a LTR: *"I met this lady at a bar and she was super nervous. There was a table full of young girls next to us and she was talking fast, knocked her glass with her hand and it broke on the floor. She gets down on her hands and knees start cleaning it up frantically, then turns around says, 'I made a mess I need a spanking.' She then asks me to go home with her on a first date."*

Jerry – 60 – in a LTR: *"I met a woman online who lived in Orlando which was an hour away from me. Though I was heading up for that way for a swing dance event and asked her if she wanted to meet me there. She agreed and said she loved to swing dance. When the woman arrived, she looked nothing like her photos. She portrayed herself as a slender, pretty lady, yet in reality she was thick and had no idea how to dance. It was like dragging a tree trunk around the floor. I told her that we will dance with multiple partners during the night and she was more than welcome to mingle with other men. I tried dancing with other women yet she would glare at anyone who would come close to me. She had a scowl on her face the entire evening and was miserable. At the end of the night she asked if she was going to see me again. I was honest and replied that I didn't feel any magic. She flipped out and said that I thought she was fat, followed by many insults and vulgar words then took off. A few weeks later the bizarre lady emails me to see we can try again. I was just honest and said sorry the magic just wasn't there."*

OVERVIEW: Rule #2

- Brush up on your dating terminology.

- Make sure you pick the right site for what you are looking for.

- Don't waste your money on paid sites; test out the free ones first and see your results.

- If you do venture onto the paid sites, do only one month at a time so you can get a good feel of the site and see if you like it prior to throwing down a lot of cash.

RULE # 3
CREATE AN ALLURING PROFILE

Now that you have decided which dating website is the best one for you, it's time to articulate what makes you stand out from the rest. It's very important you keep your profile honest, short and to the point. This isn't the time to write a novel. People have short attention spans. You want to keep it clear and concise by utilizing short paragraphs. It's easier for the eye to read that way. It should only take 60 seconds for someone to breeze over your profile and know if they want to initiate contact with you. Everyone is busy and time is of the essence.

Qualities that you should list within your profile:

1. What you are looking for? A long term relationship, just dating, friends, hook-up, marriage material-- whatever your end goal is.
2. What do you do for a living?
3. Are you single, separated, divorced, or widowed?

4. Do you have any children? If so, how many and how old? Fulltime custody or part time?
5. What kind of hobbies do you have?
6. Do you travel or have you been to other countries? If so, which ones?
7. What religion are you? Do you practice or go to church regularly? Do you want someone who does the same? Or is religion not important to you?
8. What makes you special and stand out from the crowd?
9. What qualities are you looking for in another person? Do you want a stay at home wife, a go getter, someone to travel with, or someone to just have fun with?
10. Do you want someone to love and support you and be by your side until the end of time?

These are the questions to answer in the "About Me" box: that large blank space that you have to fill in, which most people don't like to do. Make sure to write at least a couple paragraphs about who you are, what makes you tick and what you are looking for. The worst thing to do is leave it blank or fill it with zzzzzzzzzzzzzzz's. When people don't take the time to fill out a little bit of information, they portray themselves as not being serious. If I took the time to fill out my profile so you can get a feel of who I am, I'm not going to respond to someone who skipped out on the homework.

Be honest in your profile; if you're not, the truth will eventually come out. Save everyone some time and just put the truth down. Also, watch your tone while you are writing it. If you have been dissed by a lot of women and put that in there, you are going to come off as angry. No one wants to date someone that has a chip on their shoulder.. Whatever you put out into the world is going to come back to you in the same fashion. If you write an angry profile about how all women are teasers and cheaters, well then don't be surprised by the kind of woman who is going to respond to that—surely not a sweet, caring, loving one because all that negativity will scare her away. If you put happy, positive messages, you will attract happy, positive people.

Also fill out the "check boxes" portion of your profile as well—all the little boxes that ask your age, height, hair color, body type, ethnicity, et cetera. Of course be honest here, too. The one thing I find men alter the most here is height. I guess people do not know how tall they are. It seems from my experience, any guy who says he is 6ft is more like 5'9." I'm 5'9" and, for a female, that's tall. I want a tall man because when I wear heels I'm going to be 6ft. So when you say you're 6ft and I come to the date expecting that, and I wear heels and tower over you, I know you lied. Find out how tall you are. It's very disappointing to show up and be taller than your date. For me, this is also a weeding out tool. I want to be able to dress up and wear heels with the man I'm going to spend the rest of my life with. Short guys don't cut it. Save us time by finding out how tall you really are because someone who's 5'7" would never even make it to my short meet-n-greet phase (that I will go over in a later chapter).

Here are some examples of what NOT to put in your profile. These are real profiles I copied from actual dating websites. I did not change anything at all—not even the typos or spelling. It's copied word for word so you can see how some people's tones are portraying them in a negative light. Brace yourself for the not so polite descriptions. You can see for yourself what kind of person they are going to attract. Make sure you are not coming off this way:

About Me

Attention: I didn't want to resort in fishing with dynomite but theres some of you women who leave me no other choice. I'm not ugly, i'm a riot of a good time and damn right i'm funny so WTF...YOUR HEAD MUST UP YOUR SHALLOW ASS. I'm *** and you don't have to like me but you will respect me. Well...come on in, take a look around, read a bit or talk whatever but you better wipe any sh!t off your flip flops..OCD thing lmao. Just maybe theres my certain type of fish that might just jump into *my boat..i dont know but anyway. My profile is to be read with SARCASM and SENSE OF HUMOR in mind. I have put up alot to compare common interest, if so...don't be shy. It also doesn't matter if your between early 20's to early 40's of age...im always game.*

One of best times i ever had in a relationship came from this pathetic, creep-fest site. Even though i could not put a ring on it, i hope to give pof another try. Maybe next time they pull that gate..i'll get 8.

LADIES...I REFUSE TO WRITE YOU ANY KIND OF "MARK TWAIN SH!T OR 50 SHADES OF GRAY" TYPE NOVEL FOR A MESSAGE BECAUSE ITS VERY LIKELY YOUR NOT GOING TO AND NEVER HAD ANY INTENT ON REPLYING BACK...OK? GOOD LUCK ON YOUR D!CK-TEASING WONDERLAND WISH LIST OF WHY YOU'LL NEVER GET OR SHOULD NOT HAVE BEEN MARRIED AND P.O.F WINDOW SHOPPING OF MEN. Just sayin.

VERY IMPORTANT INFO!: TAKE CHANCES...because you never know how great i could turn out to be....I wasn't sure what to put down for intent so im explaing it here...I would like to GET TO KNOW AS A FRIEND and HANG OUT CASUALY or DATE a really genuine,cool,fun,funny,woman that could turn into LONG TERM OR MARRIAGE. I would like to get married..i don't believe in divorce so i'd like to make the best choice possible. Im a PICKY and i know what i want..theres certain qualities or flaws that im lookin for in a woman that i can not overlook or live with or without. I want someone that i find myself ATTRACTED to(PERFECT combination of personality and looks), is understanding(a must, cause i live in a REAL world with REAL problems),trustworthy with my HEART(again a must),patient and has a big enough heart to love and see an imperfect person perfectly. I'm the farthess from perfect but maybe i'm close enough for you. To handle me; as i found out, is going to take a perfect match. NO SAINT HERE.

PLEASE READ: If you don't go to bars wether looking foot not? Beef o bradys is a bar..Applebees is a bar...pretty much everywhere to even eat is a bar so i don't understand you...if you mean you don't drink and you hang around coffee shops with a book,ipad and iphone for fun all day, then yea we wouldn't have much to do together...SORRY MOVE ON CAUSE I KNOW HOW TO HAVE A GOOD TIME. A park with your kids is perfectly fine by me so don't get me TWISTED. Clubs is a different story..which i understand.. i dont do many "clubs" often. But if a WOMAN is out doing the same things i like doing whatever that may be and we meet then great! Im NOT sayin im NOT open to doing new things with you, which online helps with that but still.

DESCRIPTION: I'm 30/40/30% rockstar/southern/crazy. I have a funny,f@#ked up sense of humor, hope you can handle that. I'm indian, irish, old fashioned and was born and raised in the shade of a Florida palm. I'd like to concentrate on gettin all my tat work i've been wanting finished...sleeves, back etc. I have a concealed weapons license. I have a wonderful family and i would like to have one of my own maybe one day.

MUSIC TASTE: anything like...98 ROCK,eagles,ccr,eminem,dr. dre.,2 pac,biggie,b. marley,jason aldean,j. cash,hank jr,g. jones,chevelle,Hollywood undead, hellyeah, damageplan, korn, audioslave, pantera, slipknot,tool,5 f.d.p,drowning pool,mudvayne,hatebreed,mushroomhead,bleeding through,lamb of god,bobaflex,limp bizkit,dropkick murphys etc.

DISLIKES: shallow or insecure people,liars,spiders,heartbreaks,hangovers,cheaters,the law,abusers of women/kids or animals,ex-boyfriend/husband drama,cold weather,wacked out religous people,banana peppers, cheap whorish perfume,mosquitos,too much make-

up,pumkin pie,diet soda.

FOR COMEDY PURPOSES ONLY LADIES: I'm into working out and tryin to look good. So are you into fitness...we'll that's great! FitNess D!CK in your mouth.

FAVOITE QUOTE: "We do not stop playing because we grow old...we grow old because we stop playing."

~

This guy has obviously been burned in the past. He didn't take the time to heal his wounds before writing this profile. I don't know any woman who would think this profile is funny when you call women dick teases. He has a lot of issues he needs to work out. It seems like he's not going to be happy with any woman because he's not happy with himself. He needs to go back to Rule #1. The profile is also way too long. I don't know who could even suffer through reading that entire thing. After the first paragraph I would have deleted/blocked him. I don't mess with crazy. Crazy can buy machine guns online without an ID.

~

About Me
Ok ill keep this simple, I would like to meet a woman and please don't take this the wrong way I don't date outside my own race. idea like a girl who's very sweet, and who has respect for herself, someone who isn't a slut and who hasn't slept with tons of guy's, has their own car and a job, and I hate to say this has maybe one child tops, I have no kids, I like kids I just can't deal with all the screaming and constant need for attention.I don't get along well with other guys so if you have male roommates keep on looking,

I don't play well with others so if you become my girl plan on making me your only guy. in return ill do the same for you, I

48

want a real relationship I'm looking for a wife I have no time for games, I don't do one night stands, I want to meet a woman who doesn't need to go out to bars clubs and shake her ass like whore to have fun; I'm not going to bars or clubs ever again. I'm into shooting guns; play station 3. lifting weights, scuba diving; camping; if you're a cranky or a **** hit the road, I've seen and played every game in the book so if you enjoy manipulating and playing games do not even attempt to write me,

I like attention I'm looking for my best friend, if you become my girl and you have a problem with a guy showing you allot of attention go away.I also like church, I'm not a Jesus freak or anything; however I do like to go some times. Also please be in good physical shape, I'm capable of allot of love so if I love someone and for our first date you want to sit in a empty ware house on a box of milk crates eating roman noodles watching a rerun of the simpson's on a black and white TV that's ok.

~

His tone is a little bit better here, but his spelling and grammar are bad. As well as the first profile, make sure you spell check and proof read your written profile. Even have a friend check it for you, get their opinion too. He definitely has insecurities when it comes to other guys. Why would you isolate the woman you are dating and not want her to have any male friends? Maybe he was cheated on. A guy not being able to have any male friends is a big red flag. He goes to church, yet calls women whores and doesn't like children's need for constant attention. He was honest about not wanting to date outside his race and there's nothing wrong with that. That's his personal choice and was upfront about it. Though, he still is not portraying himself as a happy, secure individual. More like a loose cannon.

~

About Me

Bipolar girl.. I would like to find love.. 33. Hi.. I am a dying romantic, maybe an extinct kind? I guess lol and ok, here comes the bomb I am bipolar (anyone still there?) but I'm not crazy, so if you're still reading this we can go deeper, its hard to find someone because of my mood swings (I don't mistreat anyone anymore, mostly myself) so I get depressed and choose to by myself. It is a difficult condition, but also most geniuses are bipolar, we are extremely creative and fun, problem is all of the sudden we get frustrated with the thousands of thoughts in our head and we shut down. Because it so hard to explain this to someone else we simply don't.

Ok now that I've explained my condition a bit, I do take medications so I am fine.. I am from brazil and visiting NY would love to stay here longer if I met someone who could understand me and accept me for who I am. Oh yea and forgot to say what I look like. If I was depressed I would say fat (haha around 165) short brown hair 5'9" lots of tattoos, if I was excited id say curvy (AHAHAHAHA) same, same same....

Don't be scared, I have a lot of love to give. Its just different ☺
~

Same goes for this profile. Great, she's being honest. But if she's on medication and she's fine, then maybe that doesn't need to go in her profile. If she really has gone through therapy and medication, she should be able to maintain herself. This could be a conversation after getting to know someone. If she hasn't been able to keep her disorder under control it will show itself in person. Furthermore, if she is still emotionally unstable, which it sounds like from her personal description of herself, she needs to go back to Rule #1 and work on herself prior to dating.

Ok, now that we have seen some examples of what NOT to put in a profile, here are some examples of good profiles. These are also real life examples, so they are not perfect, but definitely a good start. Just remember to keep it short, sweet and to the point:

About Me

I am a single parent (6'2") and raising my beautiful daughter. I love the beach, parks and being on the trail enjoying the nature. I like to visit festivals, concerts, sport events. I don't like smoky bars and night clubs anymore it's over dated now, other than birthday events. I work smart and make time for the good things in life. When I go out I prefer dinner, comedy clubs and plays and concerts with my lady. I do love dancing. Being lack of that special lady I do these with friends for now. When I am involved with someone I enjoy spending time with other couples vs. my single friends. What I do for fun is not as important as who I am doing it with!!! I am member of 5 different gyms. Those places are my social environments. It gives me the opportunity to do variety of exercises and interact with completely different people and learn everyday something new. I love weekend trips and travel. I also like to stay home and watch shows and movies and cook delicious dinner but I prefer to enjoy things with my lady together. That would add even more fun for the home environment like... dance and laugh, cuddle, and have conversations. I love outdoor activities, water, mountains, and beach.I am a hard worker and have set goals. I am here to find a partner for life. I am a hopeless romantic and believe in love. Mutual respect, trust, attraction and a unique connection to making love must be present. We need to able to talk just about anything and have fun together....we can work out the rest. I am open to find love with the person who has great family values.

~

You can tell from this profile right off the bat he's a single parent, what his hobbies are, that he's into fitness and what he's looking for in a mate. He's clear, concise and to the point. It would be easy for a female to be able to read this and understand what he is looking for.

~

About Me

Looking for the perfect match for me and I for them. I want something that will turn into a long term relationship. Though, you have to date casually until you find the missing peanut butter for your jelly sandwich. I am divorced without any children.

I believe in the 80/20 rule for everything in life. I work hard and I'm driven, yet I like to have time to play as well. I still like having a few drinks and hitting the dance floor, but not every night of the week. I want to take vacations just for the fun of it on the spur of the moment.

I work out five days a week and eat healthy. On the weekends I want to splurge on a piece of cheesecake or drink beer and eat pizza. Life is too short to diet 24-7 you still have to enjoy the little things.

I'm a creative person as I enjoy writing, drawing, painting and photography. Though, I use the right and left side of my brain. I have an organized creative energy. I can be immersed for hours in a new piece of artwork and then my computer breaks. I switch gears, trouble shoot, take apart my PC and install a new graphics card. I can flip my energies like a switch when needed.

I'm looking for a man with the same multi-talented, multi-

dimensional qualities. Or at least be able to understand mine. I march to the beat of my own drum. Being a peg in a corporate wheel never worked for me nor people telling me what to do. I'm very independent yet can mesh well with anyone. I have friends of every race, creed and religion. I'm very open minded person and would like someone to be the same. I want a relationship where we choose to be with one another, not that we need each other. Two whole beings happy with their lives wanting to share it with someone else.

~

It's clear, concise and to the point. This profile is very genuine and well written. I've discovered that the more articulate you are in your own profile, the more intelligent people will be drawn to it because they will value that aspect.

Use Good, In Focus, Recent Photos

This part cannot be reinforced enough since it is one of the most abused rules in the online dating world. I'm sure you have fallen victim to it as well. You start chatting with this hot girl online and set up a date to take her out. You go into the restaurant, look around, but don't see her anywhere. Then, what appears to be, her evil, overweight twin approaches you. Appalled, you want to ask if she ate the girl with whom you were chatting online with, because it doesn't look like her at all.

I just don't understand why people post photos of themselves that do no truly represent themselves. Eventually everyone is going to find out. If you ever meet someone in person, they will find out and they're going to be upset. Unless you want to just keep it to cyber dating.

On the other hand, some people think their photos do represent them honestly. They need a wakeup call. If your photo is more than six months old, take a new one. Yes, you may still look the same, but just in case, take some new ones anyway. Sometimes we do not always see what we want to in the mirror, like those nasty 15 pounds that somehow crept onto our thighs when we were not looking. I took a photo of my friend one day with my iPhone just goofing around. When he looked at it he said, "I don't look like that! My face isn't that chubby!" Um, yeah it is. Photos don't lie! Take new ones.

These are my tips to keep your photos real and represent yourself:

1. Take one up close facial photo for your main profile photo.
2. Take one full length body shot, head to toe, by yourself.
3. Make sure they are within the last 3-6 months old.
4. Only upload in focus photos, utilizing a flash if needed.
5. Women, do not wear clothing that is too revealing or low cut; leave something to the imagination.
6. Guys, you can leave out the shirtless photos and flexing ones.
7. Don't upload photos with you and five friends. Which one are you? The other people distract from the person we want to see, which is *you*.
8. Don't do bathroom mirror shots. No one wants to see your bathroom, especially if it's dirty.
9. Do smile in your photos, brush your teeth beforehand, comb your hair and do your makeup! This is a first impression; make it a good one.
10. Do post photos of you engaging in your hobbies; how do you like to have fun?
11. Do post photos of your furry friends. If your pets are more like family, you'll want to know someone will accept them too.
12. If you're a woman, don't upload photos with you and a ton of men and the same goes for guys. What are you trying to prove? How many guys/girls you can snag?

13. Don't post photos of your children. I personally think your children should stay private. You never know the weirdoes/ stalkers on internet dating sites. Do mention that you have kids in your bio section.
14. If you do not have children, don't post photos of you and a baby. I've seen a lot of this and it's confusing. If I see a man in a photo with a newborn, I'm assuming he has children.

If you can, have a family member or friends help take some photos of you. It's always good to get someone else's opinion, too. If you don't feel comfortable with that, you can always find a professional photographer. If you live in the Tampa Bay area I do offer photo packages. If you live elsewhere there are usually lots of photographers available for shoots. You always want to include a photo in your profile. In this day and age of smart phones, iPads, and digital cameras, there's really no excuse to not have one. It also helps in the initial weeding out process. Don't you want to go on a date with someone who's at least somewhat initially attracted to you? I'm sorry, but no one's personality can shine *that* well through a two-paragraph personal essay. A photo says a thousand words.

My experiences with people who do not have photos on their profiles are either married or butt ugly. Some say they do it for their privacy. Well, if you want privacy then don't be using an online dating site! Don't let someone get away with emailing you a photo, either. They need to put their photo on their profile. If they refuse, they are trying to hide something or hide from someone. One guy said to me he didn't have any photos of himself. Really? No photos at all? What are you in the witness protection program? Come on, I wasn't born yesterday. I told him to go to Kinko's, take a passport photo and then have them scan it in as a.jpg file. Needless to say, I never heard from him again.

Choose a Catchy Username & Headline

Your username and headline is like your own personal elevator pitch and tagline. What is your business model? How can you sum yourself up in one sentence? Some people just use their name, some are funny and others are, well just freaky. Spend some time to come up with a username that describes you best. Choose wisely, you may not receive responses if are condensing or sexual. I will not reply to someone who has a headline of: More like Plenty of Whores!! Yes, that it a real headline someone has on POF.com. Need I say more? Here are examples of bad/ funny usernames:

1. Herebecauseofmyx
2. Stupidbuthopeful
3. Hotdong357
4. PizzaTaxi
5. slacker775
6. Time2PlayNice
7. Whywhywhy
8. Luveher2nite
9. YouBetterPickMe
10. Dumbblondee
11. Porcupinecuddles , Headline: Don't get too close
12. Horney 479
13. Barstoolsailor
14. Fukthoseguys
15. Mcfartpants
16. Iwontmurderyou
17. Meatstick

Funny Dating Story

On a Tuesday night, I went out for a couple of drinks at a local tavern with some friends. I had been chatting online with a guy and he asked me what I was doing that night, so I asked him if he wanted to meet us out for a drink. His profile only had one picture of a rugged, curly haired man wearing a suit. The rest of his profile was pretty much the same song and dance as most others. He agreed to meet us at 8 p.m. My friends and I arrived at 7:30 and at 8:15 he texted and said he was on his way. I was having a good time listening to music and having great conversations. Thirty minutes later, my phone lit up; he said he was there. I looked around but didn't see anyone. He continued to hide and text me from afar. I wasn't up for a game of cat and mouse, so my friend went to see if he was actually there. My friend noticed him from afar, but he still didn't approach me. I saw him go off to the restroom, so I decided to confront him once he came out.

As I stood there, thinking of all the things I wanted to vent as to why he was being so shady, the door opened. When he walked out I was speechless. His face explained it all. All my built up frustration melted away and sadness took its place. I was stunned and didn't know what to say. Instead of my plan of attack, I backed down and asked why he hadn't come over to say hi. As he told me some excuse, all his words fell on deaf ears. He was talking, but I was trying to grasp all the scars on his face. Multiple lacerations and deep wounds ran up and down the facial bones. His eyes were not quite aligned and one was more prominent than the other—like a porcelain Greek statue shattered and glued back together. He limped over to the table to sit with me and my friends. We made small talk, but no one brought up the elephant in the room. I finally asked if he had been in an accident, because I couldn't hold it in any longer. He began to tell me of a horrific car accident he was in. His speech was slurred while he told the gruesome story, yet he had not been drinking any alcohol. He's lucky to be alive. I felt like I was in my own version of Vanilla Sky, trying to see the man for who he was behind all the scars. Though what kept going through my mind was: *Why wouldn't he have said something to this effect in his online dating profile?* There's no check box asking if you've been disfigured in an accident, yet that's something you should mention, along with posting current photos of your condition so you can find someone sympathetic to your situation.

Never misrepresent yourself in your profile. It may be difficult if you've been in an accident, had surgery or something else, but not portraying yourself honestly isn't going to work either. Telling the truth from the beginning is going to help in the weeding out process. Why would you want to be with someone who doesn't accept you for who you truly are? That's why you need clear photos. Not everyone is going to be attracted to everyone else, that's life. Accept yourself, be happy and put yourself out there. You will find someone who admires that and will be happy with the real you. I myself am tall and very muscular, so a man looking for an anorexic super model or petite lady would not be attracted to me. If he doesn't like a woman with a sizeable ass, then we are not meant to be. It's okay though, it only takes one wonderful person to spend the rest of your life with.

From the Y Chromosome

1) What do you think are the best elements in a good profile?

Nathan – 28 – Single: *"I had professional photos taken for my profile. I think it's better to have someone else take photos of you. I don't like it when the girls take self-portrait shots with their smart phone from high up because it makes them look skinny when they're really fat. Match.com has a feature where they will revise your profile for $40, but all they do is move stuff around and it doesn't do anything."*

Dan – 56 – in a LTR: *"I had two good photos taken. The first one I was wearing a white dress shirt and blazer on, more professional looking close up shot. The second photo was of me out in the woods wearing jean cutoffs, a cool t-shirt leaning on a tree showing me head to toe. So when you looked at my profile you saw me in a classy and then rugged way. I don't think you need tons of photos on your profile like some women display, two is good enough.*

In my written section I put that I was five years younger than what I was. I did that for a purpose because I'm young at heart and love going to live concerts and listening to AC/DC. All the women over 50 are boring and they don't like to do the same things that I do. I also stated that I had been married for four years and divorced when in reality I have not been married yet. For some reason there's a stigma attach to bachelors that are over 50. If I was honest in my profile then women wondered what was wrong with me. I would tell them the truth once we met in person though.

On POF.com they have a question about what you would do on a first date. I wrote this great essay that was similar to: I will pick you up in a limo to my personal jet to fly to Rio de Janeiro and enjoy the beaches, then for lunch fly over to a little café in Paris. For dessert I will whisk you to a romantic hotel on the Amalfi coast of Italy, where the ocean breeze would ruffle our satin bed sheets. Women loved it! Some emailed me to ask if that's what I would really do, of course I wouldn't."

Chris – 41 – Divorced: *"I just try to show that I'm active and decent guy, not a creepy, old, fat man. But it's hard to get women's attention. I don't like women that have half naked photos or ones of them in bikinis. I think it puts them in a negative light. Show's they have low self-esteem. I would rather see a professional photo like them at work and then some of them out with friends. If they have a fake looking photo then it's probably a fake profile."*

Jerry – 60 – in a LTR: *"Most importantly be honest with yourself and what you're looking for. Don't post naked photos or cut out other people from them. Not appropriate to put photos of your children on dating sites, just mention that you have kids in your written bio. Don't conventionally leave out essential information like you're missing a leg or arm. It's not good to talk about past relationships or bash your ex. I would tell dates that I had a friendly divorce but women didn't want to hear about it. Definitely avoid typing in all capital letters; I don't like to be yelled at. Try to be more positive instead of listing out all the things you don't want in a person in bullet points."*

OVERVIEW: Rule #3

- In your profile be honest, short, sweet, and to the point.
- Take current photos: at least one upfront, one close facial and one full length body photo.
- Don't lie in your profile; eventually everyone's going to find out the truth. Start by being honest and find someone who loves you for you.

RULE #4
INITIATING CONTACT ONLINE

Once you've decided on a website that's right for you and created your profile, now it's time to start chatting! Some people think that it's a numbers game, email as many people as you can and see who responds. I don't think this is a concrete way to find someone that you actually are interested in. You need to read the profiles of people *prior* to emailing them. Nothing is more annoying than getting a bulk email from someone on a dating site. You can identify this love spam by the way the email is so generalized. If it doesn't say anything as to why you stood out from the crowd such as: "I love the fact that you published a book" and is more like: "You are so gorgeous," then its love spam!

I just recently discovered from a male friend, who is involved with online dating and has read some of the crazy emails I receive from guys, that there is actually sites out there with email templates. If you don't know what to say to someone online you can just copy and paste these templates and insert your personal information. This could be all the "love spam" I receive. I recommend not utilizing these prototypes. You can use them as a guide, but come up with your own stuff. A short personalized email is going to get you a much higher response rate versus love spam.

As your browsing profiles and you see someone interesting, make sure to read *all* of their profile. It's okay to be initially attracted by someone's photos. There's nothing wrong with that. We all need to be physically attracted to someone in order to have chemistry or in-between the sheets action. Once you do find someone you're attracted to, read all their bullet points and all of their bio. Sometimes I find I may be attracted to their photos and then turned off by reading their profile if they come off as angry, too controlling or insecure. If you decided, after reading everything, you want to send them an email, pick out something special you liked. Make the email personalized towards them. That will more than likely initiate a response back. They will be touched that you actually read their profile.

I conducted an experiment on OkCupid to see how many people actually read someone's full bio prior to initiating contact. I wasn't sure how to pull this off at first, then while I was filing out the profile on OkCupid, I decided to add this at the very end of my profile, "If you read my whole profile and didn't just look at my photos, enter this captcha in your contact email: < (^^) >".

After conducting my experiment based on 138 emails sent to me, 60 percent of those did not contain any captcha or mention of it. So that means only 40 percent of men actually read an entire profile prior to sending an email. A few said they refused to type it or couldn't figure out how to recreate it, though at least they mentioned it, so means the read all the way through. Actually utilizing this captcha was helpful to me. If a person did not enter it, I wouldn't respond because I knew they were not serious. It helped weed out the guys not interested in *really* getting to know me. Some still turned out weird after the fact, yet it was a smaller number compared to if I just responded to everyone in general.

Examples of Bad Introductory Emails

Let me remind you as you read these, that they are *real* emails coming from *real* people on *real* dating sites. These are examples of what *not* to send to a potential date:

I'd hit that. ~ I don't think I need to explain, but obviously don't send an email like this unless you are looking for a one night stand. Emails I receive similar to this result in that user being blocked from my account.

Good Morning Beautiful. ~ Some people may think there's nothing wrong with an email like this. It's sweet and genuine, yes, but not for an introductory email. This is more like an email or text message a boyfriend/girlfriend would send after dating for a few months. As an intro email it comes off as cheesy. How many times can you copy and paste that to how many women or men?

U look great u got my attention. ~ This email is even cheesier than the one prior. First of all, I may be picky being a writer and all, but use proper grammar. I know in this day and age of texting, tweeting and pinning, everyone uses short hand, but when composing an email, spell it out! Also he's only portraying here that he noticed my photos, fantastic. What about my bio? Does he know anything about me or is he just looking for arm candy? Sorry, I'm not looking to be someone's trophy wife.

Hey there, so my friend and I have a bet going that your profile isn't real. I think it is because your "about me" seems realistic. So I've got $20 riding on this now... don't let me down. ~ Yeah, obviously a bet between two buddies isn't a way to start a conversation.

Hey what's up? I had to say hi. You're so damn fine. Those hips those thighs. Ever had a sexy chocolate kiss from a thug? ~ Um... I don't make out with gang bangers and I don't want to start now.

Thought I would of heard from you by now? When do you want to talk? Let me know when and if you want to talk? I am a night owl too. Let's hit a hot VIP event or party together and have FUN! 532-3156 or send me yours. ~ This email screams douche bag. If you could have seen the photos that went along with it (I obviously can't print them for privacy reasons.) Every photo was of him with a celebrity, like he needs celebrity endorsement to get a date. Then he says that I should have contacted *him*? Can we say cocky?? Who is he? Definitely not that important or famous if he's on Plenty of Fish dating site. I don't think famous people need a dating site. All he wants is a party girl and probably a one night stand. Never send someone your phone number in the first email either. It comes off as desperate in my eyes. Don't you want to chat first and get to know me? Or do you just love spam every chick on the site with your cell number. Ewwww-- like phone STDs.

Are you the one? ~ Nope, obviously not.

I'm never this forgetful, but I forgot what time we were supposed to meet tonight? 7:15 or 8:30? ~ Okay we never had a date set up, so don't pretend we had a date.

Hello there my dear, like a piece of artwork being unveiled.. those are the only words I can use to describe your pictures my dear. Please tell me my dear.. where have you been all my life? Been looking for you in the day and night with a flash light. P.S. I can erase the past. ~ Hmmm sounds like a long cheesy bar pick up line. How do you know I'm the one just from my photos and we have never met in person or even spoken on the phone? It's over the top and not sincere since he has no idea who I am.

Hi there, saw your profile and wanted to ask you something, will you marry me? ~ Marriage proposals are not acceptable as first email material. I'm sure he's trying to come off as funny, but I think it's kind of creepy.

I have a job, but no longer have a car as of now I live in a one bedroom apartment with my mom i sleep on the sofa cause i can not afford to live alone right now. Being honest here, do I even have a chance? ~ No, you do not have a chance. This guy needs to get his life organized first. You should not be out dating if you can't even meet a girl for a first date. This is clearly Puppy Dog Syndrome Rule #5 from my first book. Taking in someone that you want to help or fix. If a woman went out with him she would be driving, probably picking up the tab and eventually getting an unwanted roommate.

Examples of Good Email Introductions

Hi, I noticed you like to go rollerblading. What trails or areas do you usually go? I really like the causeway during sunset. Would you like to go rollerblading together sometime? ~ This email is sincere. You can tell they read your profile because they mentioned that you like rollerblading. Right there the two of you have something in common you can have a conversation about. They are asking you out but in a non-pressure kind of way.

Hi how's your evening? I see you're a real estate agent. Do you concentrate on residential or commercial? ~ Asking someone a question about their career is going to trigger a response. Most people would feel compelled to respond because you're starting a conversation. It's again low pressure, non-cheesy and you would feel the need to tell them more specifically what you do. On another note, I have made business contacts on dating sites. Nice people that there just wasn't any chemistry, but yet we continued a friendship and then business evolved.

Hot versus Beautiful

When you start conversing with someone online, be careful of the words you choose to chat with them. Especially since terminology can be misconstrued via emails. You don't know how they will interpret something. You may try to be funny and they think you're rude.

For example, hot versus beautiful. These two words have very different meanings and different connotations. I had a discussion with a man I dated, who was also a writer, about how these words used as adjectives to describe women have varied results. When a man refers to me as *hot*, I get the sense that he basically only cares about my outer appearance and his basic goal is just to get me into bed. *Hot* refers to more of a sexual desire or longing for a woman. Whereas if a man calls me *beautiful*, it makes me feel that he desires my brain, personality, and overall being as well as my looks. You can be *beautiful* inside and out. I'm not sure if you can be *hot* inside and out. I suppose you could if you have the flu and a fever over 100 degrees. Though, that wouldn't be very attractive to anyone.

Pay attention to the verbiage you use. I get turned off when a guy's first email to me on an internet dating website is, "Wow you're so hot." Okay great, but did you even take the time to read my profile? Of course you can compliment a woman, but we want to know you care more about what's on our inside versus what's on the outside. Start the conversation by talking about something she's interested instead of her appearance. Taking the time to find out what she's into shows you care more about her than just getting into her pants and that will win you points.

The Weeding Out Process Online

If you are a half way decent looking guy or girl, you are going to receive anywhere from 20 to 50 emails a day. It can become overwhelming. You do not want to spend your entire day emailing everyone back. The good ones are going to get lost in the shuffle with the bad ones.

Devise a plan of attack. Check your email two - three times a day. Each time you check the online account, have at least five non-negotiables in mind. What are the qualities in another person that you just can't live without? Don't go overboard, remember, this is just an initial weeding out process. For example, these are my non-negotiables when I filter through emails:

1) They have to be between the ages of 25 and 45.
2) I don't want to date anyone right now that currently has children under 18 years old.
3) They must live within a 50 mile radius from me (no long distance relationships).
4) They cannot be legally bound to another person (separated but not divorced).
5) No one under 6ft tall (I'm very tall, so short guys do not work for me).
6) Must have full-time employment (either self-employed or work for someone).
7) I have to be attracted to their photos.
8) Their email and profile must be articulate and doesn't say something like, "Hey sexy momma."

This is the first step in deciding who you want to email back. When you open an email, read it, check their profile against your criteria. Does it meet all standards? If one thing is off, skip, onto the next! Be concrete with what your non-negotiables are. Don't waiver from them. If you don't want to date someone with kids, then no matter how cute the guy or girl is, move on. If one of your requirements is someone who is thin and not overweight that's fine. Some our desires are superficial and that's ok. As long they not *all* of them are. Let's be honest here, you need to be physically attracted to someone in order to be in an intimate relationship. As much as it would be nice to say you're only attracted to their personality, if they weigh 400 pounds and have a snaggle tooth, sweetness isn't going to make a huge impact. Don't beat yourself up about it. It's a crucial part of the dating process. Someone may have all the qualities you want but there's just no chemistry. You think you should be attracted to this person, what's wrong with me? Don't beat yourself up about it. If all the pieces don't fit into the puzzle, move on until there's someone that does. There's someone out there for everyone. The 400 pound snaggle tooth person will find love and so will you.

When you check their profile make sure to read the entire entry before responding. If you don't, you may miss something listed within the content that was against your non-negotiables. Also, pay attention to the tone of the message. From my experience, it seems there are a lot of irate people on these sites who are pissed off for one reason or another. I came across a guy's profile that was mostly in all caps (online yelling) and saying rude remarks to all women in general. When you come across someone that looks like a loose cannon or sends you a rude email, don't even respond. You don't want to piss off a psycho. Better to defuse the situation. Any response you send is going to give them ammunition. In this day and age you don't want to mess with irrational people, because they might be able to internet stalk you and find out where you live. .

If the person doesn't seem like a psycho killer, it is nice to send a short courteous email just stating that you're not interested. I've discovered that if you don't respond at all to someone's email then they think it may have been deleted or lost in the shuffle. Some may become very determined and will continue to email you endlessly until they receive a response. Example of a short email to let someone know you're not interested:

"Hello, thanks for your email. After looking at your profile I do not think we would be a good match. I appreciate your interest and good luck with your search!"

It's sincere, short and to the point. Most people should respect that you're being honest with them. Some will freak out or be irrational, you do not have to respond to them. You've already stated your opinion. If they continue to email you, then you just have to block them. Don't engage in fighting over the internet. You may think you're safe behind your computer screen or that it's just between you and that one person.

Within my group of girlfriends and guy friends who are single in the Tampa Bay dating jungle, we compare notes. We look at each other's dating profiles and see who each other to talking to and sharing our experiences. So, if you think being a dick or psycho chick to one person isn't a big deal, think again. You may get a reputation in the online dating jungle that you can't shake.

On the other end of the spectrum, if you are the one sending emails out to someone and they don't respond, after two attempts STOP. I know we should all have good morals and values to email everyone back, but a lot don't. For the most part it's just a time issue. It's hard to filter through 50 emails in a day. After working fulltime, driving in traffic to and from work, when you're home you're tired and just want to relax. After two attempts at contacting someone who does not respond, just chalk it up to that they are not interested for one reason or another. If you continuously email repeatedly without a response, you come off as desperate and needy. Both of which are bad qualities. Now you just ruined your chances of *ever* talking to them again.

Who knows, maybe they were out of town, had no internet access or their computer was at the store being worked on. If and when they do get to their inbox and see a slew of emails from you, now they are thinking psycho stalker. Make two attempts but leave it at that.

Exchanging Personal Phone Numbers

At some point you are going to want to take your online romance offline. I will go into more detail about that in the next chapter. The step before meeting in person is taking it from the dating site to a more personal level. Some people want to do it as soon as possible. I guess it depends upon how comfortable you feel with that person. It is much easier to text versus logging onto a website to send an email. Though, be careful with your phone number. You don't want to just give it out to anyone and everyone.

I treat my cell phone number as a privilege that only a few elite will get. Men are lot more frivolous with this. Even being a man you shouldn't throw your phone number out to everyone woman on every dating site. You don't know who is psycho or crazy. Especially don't send your phone number out in the very first initial email. It's really weird to open an email from a complete stranger you have never had a conversation with and they are willing to put their cell number out there. It screams desperate. How many other people have you thrown your number to? You wouldn't even know who it is calling you. You don't know my name, I barely know you and you want to get random texts and phone call from a women who could be crazy?

Sending everyone your cell in a first email is like throwing mud at the wall and seeing where it sticks. Not very romantic on the receiving end. It also makes me think how many other people have you sent it to? Was I number 10 or 50 on your list? Wait until you've gotten to know someone well or at least think you would like to get to know better prior to exchanging phone numbers. If you don't, this could happen to you:

Funny Dating Story

Sometimes online dates self-destruct before you can even meet in person. I flew home to Nebraska for Christmas during 2012 and was sick before I left the sunny 80 degree weather to enter into a blizzard. I arrived on a Friday, yet stayed inside cozy next to the fireplace working on my book and trying to get better before the holiday festivities started. In-between editing my book I was chatting with a few guys from POF. I had narrowed it down to a couple guys that stood out and two of them asked for my phone number. I was reluctant as always giving out my digits, though I made them promise to not text stalk me if I did. They obliged and texting began. Since I had just arrived in the Midwest, I wouldn't be back for a week to actually meet anyone in person.

The one guy younger, good looking, ex-army was very persistent. He would call and text. We had a few hour long conversations and for the first three days I thought he might be someone I could really like once I got back to Florida. He came off as intelligent, hardworking and really had his shit together for being younger than myself. 'Twas the night before Christmas when it all fell apart. Utter melt down at O 200 hours. I had just settled down for a long winter's nap, when my cell phone arose me with such a clatter. I sprang from the bed to see what was the matter. Multiple texts telling me he doesn't have a car, he's broke, no family to spend the holidays with and was lonely. I responded to try to reassure him everything would be ok and went back to sleep placing my phone on silent mode.

The next morning I awoke to four missed phone calls and text messages. I respond with one short text and before it even goes through he's calling me back. I answered, freshly out of bed and groggy. He starts rambling on in a condescending tone, "Merry Christmas, can you hear all the spoiled brats unwrapping their Christmas presents?" He continues on to ask me what I'm doing for New Year's Eve, I'm I going to come visit him at the bar he's bouncing that night? I said no I have plans with friends to go to a fancy masquerade that I have already bought tickets to. He responds, "Who am I going to make out with at midnight then!?"

Next morning he's calling/ texting obsessively and I only responded a few times. At night he texts again that he drove a friend's car to a bar and is getting drunk. He's depressed and sad. I tell him to go home and sleep it off, to take a taxi he shouldn't be driving a friend's car drunk. He tells me not to be mean, he doesn't need it. The next morning he texts me with nothing but ☹ sad faces. I decide I shouldn't respond to him anymore.

The bad thing with giving out your phone number and someone

starts stalking you is, it costs money to change your phone number and for some reason you cannot block numbers. I really wish they could change this. I have an iPhone and have tried to download apps to block numbers, yet to no avail nothing I have discovered works. So when someone goes crazy, you have to just ignore them, which can be hard to do. Especially if they are obsessive compulsive. During the separation phase with my ex-husband I had to turn my phone off he was so bad. When I did turn my phone back on I had 50 missed calls and 10 voicemails. I ended up changing my cell phone number and AT&T charged me $50. Not a cheap thing to do and a pain in the butt especially if you use your cell for business purposes. You can set up google numbers which is helpful in the beginning of a relationship. It's free and it will be forwarded to your cell phone. Visit www.google.com/voice to set it up. It's very easy and user friendly. I wish I would have now with Mr. Meltdown.

Don't Send Naked Photos

Now that you have the privilege of someone giving you their phone number, don't abuse it. Don't send naked photos! I can't tell you how many times I have given out my cell phone number or private email address to then be sent photos of their penis. The last thing I want to see at 9am as I'm sipping my coffee, reading through my emails is a picture of someone's genitals pop up. I really don't understand why men feel the need to do this? Is it the virtual way of flashing? Do they get off on this? It makes me block and never speak to them again. I could literally publish an entire book and call it, "Penis' of the Internet".

I know some women do this as well. Send full naked body shots to guys they met online. This is the way you get booty calls at 2am, not a way to find a long term relationship. Once you're committed to someone you can do whatever kind of foreplay you want. Not before you've even met the guy in person. Plus why would you send incriminating evidence to someone you barely know? He's probably passing it round the office! You want to get a reputation as that kind of girl? Have some respect for yourself and your body. Save it for someone special that deserves it.

Also don't ask constantly for a picture of the other person. It's so annoying when a guy constantly asks me to send him photos of myself. Then they want sexy ones. No, I'm not going to pose like a whore with a fish face to make you happy. I'll send one nice photo so you can put it in your contact information on your phone. If you want to see a better close up of me, meet me in person.

Sexting

When you're first covering with someone from online, leave the sexual messages at the door. It's rude from a woman's point of view to send her sexual innuendos, especially when you haven't met in person yet. This means you are only looking for a hook-up and don't care about us as human beings. Same goes for women sending sexually explicit text messages to men. They may like it, but they are not going to respect you at the end of the day as an intelligent person.

Sending dirty messages to a stranger that makes their iPhone blush is not smart. Something to keep in mind is that sexting is now considered a sexual crime. Child pornography and misdemeanor is what you can be charged with if you engage in sexting if you are under age or the person you're conversing with is. Computer cameras that allow you to video stream or video chat are also included.

Many adults participate in sexting, some very graphic with people they have never met in person. You have no idea who the other person is on the receiving end of that message. It could be a teenager who exaggerated their age in an online profile. I know I always looked older than my real age when I was growing up. When I was 14 years old I looked 19. Lots of time girls pretend to be older than what they really are. This is just another reason not to send photos of your genitalia.

From the Y Chromosome

1) What usually makes you initiate contact online to a woman?

Nathan – 28 – Single: *"I believe the man should initiate first contact online. If the woman doesn't respond then I'll email again in a week. Sometimes I'll receive a response the second time, if I don't then after two emails I'll leave her alone. It all of course depends upon if you're on a paid site or not and if that other person has paid. I'll also look to see when the last time they were online. If someone's account hasn't been active for days then they are probably not too active on there and I may not email them. I do sometimes receive emails from women initially yet it's never anyone I like. I do prefer chatting with someone through the IM feature versus sending emails, though it's hard to get a conversation going that way sometimes."*

Dan – 56 – in a LTR: *"When I'm looking at profiles to see who to email the first thing I look at is their photos. Then I check to see their size I like petite, thin women with small breasts. I will thirdly check where they are located and if it's close to me, then see how her family life is. If a women says or has photos with her and a tons of animals there's no way I'm contacting her, because she's lonely and needs all those animals around to make her feel good. No cussing in profiles I do not appreciate that, women should not swear. I couldn't be with a type A personality because I am. I'm more traditional in the sense that I'm the man and she's the woman. Though, it doesn't matter to me if women have half naked photos online or not I'll still email them if I like them."*

Chris – 41 – Divorced: *"I look at photos first then I read their profiles. Then onto their height, age, if they have kids, and then question portion on OkCupid to see what we have in common. If I decide to email them I* *will point out things we both like to do. I also look at the username they chose so it's not something weird like: SpoiledRUs."*

Jerry – 60 – in a LTR: *"I see their photos first. I like very slender women, I know is superficial but it's just what I like. I also look for the "wow" factor. Something that makes them stand out and makes me really says "wow" out loud. It could be: talent, looks, education, or just extraordinary. I like it when women have nice photos of them smiling. A close up and a faraway to show your body type, have someone else take a photo of you. Stay away from group photos it makes it hard to find out which person is the one I'm emailing.*

I would maybe receive 5-10 emails a week from women. I was on 3-5 different sites at the same time. Most women would write me when I was very specific of what I wanted in my profile. I believe the more detailed you are in what you are looking for in your bio, the less responses you will receive, yet they will be what you want. Sometimes I would get nasty grams from ladies, yet I'm very honest in what I'm looking for, I know what I want."

OVERVIEW: Rule #4

- Don't send love spam. Read their profile and ask them a question specific to their interests.
- Stick to your 5 non-negotiables to weed out potential dates online first.
- Don't exchange phone numbers until you know it's someone you truly want to get to know better.
- If the relationship goes south, don't phone stalk the other person, save your dignity.

RULE #5
WHEN TO TAKE IT OFFLINE

Finally, you meet someone online that you really like. You've been chatting for a while and it seems you have a connection, online at least. The two of you have exchanged phone numbers and have had a few conversations. You like the sound of their voice and now you're more intrigued than ever to meet your budding online romance. Now it's time to take it offline and meet in person.

Within two weeks of chatting with someone online you need to set up a short meet-n-greet. Do not wait longer than two weeks unless for some reason your schedules conflict. There's a reason behind this two week time frame. I've been stuck in virtual romances that lasted months without ever meeting the other person. I had no idea what they looked like in person. When I forced the issue and set up a time and date, they canceled at the last minute. I never did meet them in person and I wasted months of my valuable time.

If someone doesn't want to meet you out in public, there's usually something wrong. Either they do not look like their photos or possibly they are married. We really don't know for sure why the other person keeps avoiding "reality" yet we do know that they are not truly representing themselves 100 percent. You don't want to be with someone who can't be honest with themselves.

The other reason for the two week timeframe is because the one thing you can never mimic over the internet or even through phone conversations is chemistry. Sure, you can text and flirt over the phone and you may like the sound of their voice, yet in person chemistry is so much more than that. There's so many moving pieces that our subconscious brain picks up on: our body language, certain movements and facial expressions. Chemistry is hardwired into our brains and I do not know if anyone really understands it. It's something that just happens when you meet someone, either it's there or it's not. There's nothing you can really do about it or even try to make happen. This person either makes happy thoughts and things happen inside of you or not.

Have you ever tried to force chemistry? Tried to make yourself like someone because your mom or your friends said "this is the one for you"? I know I have and it's never worked. Sure, this guy is great on paper and everyone says I should go for him. He's got a great job, nice car, great education, good looking, but he doesn't do anything for me. Yes, I have gone on dates with that kind of person and even tried to force a relationship, yet it never works out. Chemistry can't be forced, it can be developed over time, but it's one of those gut instincts. You can feel it deep down inside of you.

I think guys may be better at this aspect versus women. From my experience, men can sense after a few seconds if they want to approach a woman or ask her out. They can tell quickly, *yeah I dig her*. With women we tend to over analyze everything, taking all different factors into some lengthy algorithm then seeing what answer spits out. We will go on a few dates. Even if we're not feeling it, if he asks for a third, we decide to give it another shot. This is insanity. Chemistry doesn't need all this thinking; it's all natural human instincts. If we stop thinking so much and start feeling instead it would make things a whole lot easier.

When we participate in a virtual romance of picture texts, phone calls and emails we start to form an idea of this person and a relationship in our head. The longer we keep it online the more we become attached to our mental image we are creating of this person. We include the entire characteristics we want in our ideal mate and relationship. Our view becomes warped and we start living in our made up la la land in our head. Everything about this person is perfect! He's tall, dresses nice, his house is always clean, and he opens the door for me and sends me flowers for no reason. The higher up we put this person on a pedestal, the farther they have to fall once we meet them in person. There's no way they will measure up to the unrealistic expectations we have created in our mind. You need to meet them in person as soon as you can so you can fall in love with who they are, not some made up dream.

Initial Meet-n-Greets

Now that we have established a time frame to take the online romance offline, here are some guidelines for initial meetings. I do not call these dates because when you are dating online you really do not know much about that person until you meet them in the flesh. No one wants to plan an all night date with a stranger who shows up looking nothing like their photos. You think you have an awesome date set up with Ms. USA and the woman who shows up instead looks like she *ate* the person you were conversing with. Unfortunately, people do misrepresent themselves online or sometimes there's just no other reason than the two of you just don't click. No harm no foul.

The first time meeting someone in person, set up a short meet-n-greet. All you really need is about 15 minutes to know if this person is someone you would like to get to know better. There's not going to be a connection with everyone. If there was, we would all be happily married with bountiful children. You may have to go on 20 short meet-n-greets before you find that special someone. That's fine, it's a process. Kind of like a job interview, yet it should be more fun.

Keep your expectations average, but not too low. You just don't want to set yourself up for failure. Don't go into the date with the mentality of: *I'm going to find my future wife/ husband*. That puts too much pressure on the entire situation and will make both of you tense. Go in with the mindset of: *today I'm going to make a great new friend*. If something more happens, fantastic! If not you can increase your network of friends/ business contacts or, who knows, maybe this person would be great for another single friend of yours. I've made great contacts and friends through short meet-n-greets. You never want to burn bridges or become known as that jerk from Plenty of Fish as we all know bad information travels quicker than good. When you have multiple friends on dating websites, we do share information and stories. So if you're a jerk to one woman don't think it's ok because you'll never see her again. That is true, but you'll never go out with all the other women she told as well. Let's be nice and treat each other with respect, it's a jungle out there and we're all just trying to survive!

Meeting for coffee is great for initial meet-n-greets. For one, it shouldn't take more than 30 minutes to drink a cappuccino. That will give you plenty of time to decide if there's something more with this person you want to pursue. If there isn't, then it's an easy way out. You have errands to run, it was nice meeting you and it was only a couple of bucks out of your pocket. I believe coffee dates are much more effective in the dating process versus happy hour dates. I know lots of people like to meet for happy hour; you're nervous and a glass of wine will calm your nerves. But alcohol, along with letting down your inhibitions, blurs your judgment. One drink turns into three or four and before you know it, you've got a great buzz going on. This guy is fantastic, or so you think. He's making you laugh; he's good looking and saying all the right stuff.

Your mind starts to swirl thinking what a cute couple the two of you make. The RSVP card with his name down as your plus one to your friend's upcoming wedding is being filled out. He walks you to your car, gives you an amazing first kiss and it makes your knees buckle. The date for tomorrow night is already being scheduled.

Next date comes, as you gaze at him from across the table, the acne on his face is way more prevalent tonight. The jokes come off as more condescending as he continuously interrupts your story. You wonder if this is an entirely different person. Nope, last night was booze induced chemistry, not real chemistry. Real chemistry happens between two people without any other recreational drugs. Though it may feel like your high, you are only high on love and isn't that the best feeling of all?

Just as alcohol lowers your inhibitions, it also blocks you from creating a healthy relationship—especially if you are having issues with finding a wholesome person to start a romance with. You cannot listen to all of your inside voices, bells, whistles and intuition. You're drowning it out with alcohol. After you get to know someone, obviously it's ok to go out for drinks or have a glass of wine with dinner. Just not in the beginning, especially not on the first date.

Always Meet in a Public Place

Since this is a blind date, and you do not know the person from the internet that you are meeting just yet, **do not have them pick you up at your house.** You want to keep your home safe from stalkers and creepy people. Plus you do not want to get stuck with someone in a car who could be mentally unstable. We all have heard of The Craigslist Killer. An American medical student who was charged with the armed robbery and murder of a woman back in 2009 and robbery of two other women he met from ads on Craigslist. You have to be careful when meeting strangers from online or anywhere for that matter. Even if you meet someone for a short meet-n-greet and then they want to go to dinner afterwards, take two separate cars. I'll usually take my own car for the first three dates, then if I feel comfortable I'll let them come and pick me up.

Pay Attention How Your Date Treats Other People

One important way to see the personality of how someone is when you first meet them, is to see how they treat other people. Of course it's important how they treat you as well, though most are on their best behavior the first few months of dating. Pay close attention to how your date treats wait staff, bar tenders, valet and other service workers. Anyone can kiss your butt and make you feel good, but how nice are they to the hostess? Do they open doors for you, kiss you on the cheek then scream at the waiter for brining Diet Coke instead of regular Coke? How someone treats less significant people in their lives shows how eventually you may be treated. Plus it's embarrassing to be with someone whose rude to others. We should all be polite and have common courtesy to others.

Funny Dating Story

One way to lose a girl in 10 minutes or less is to be a total dick. I'm not talking about being a dick to your date, but to everyone else involved within the date. Such as servers, bartenders, hostess etc. It's really not attractive to treat them like the scum of the earth or your servants to impress a girl. It is downright insulting and a girl who likes that isn't a nice person to begin with. You can kiss my butt all night long, but what I really pay attention to is how do you treat everyone else?

I was appalled at the behavior of one man I met of POF. He started off by being 15 minutes late to begin with. Strike #1. I had a glass of wine at the bar waiting for him to arrive. As I sat I chit chatted with all the bartenders who were very nice and gave great customer service. As soon as my date arrived I was surprised by his appearance because he didn't look anything like his photo. Somehow within an hour of seeing his profile online to meeting in person, he had gone bald with a last few hairs grey. Strike #2.

As we waited for the "prime" table, even though numerous others were available, he yelled at one bartender to cash us out while she had her back turned to us obviously taking care of another customer. When she did not immediately comply, he turned to another and banged his credit card loudly on the table until she acknowledged him. I was so embarrassed I wanted to dig a hole and crawl in it so no one would see me with such an asshole. Strike #3.

Once we were seated he started the conversation by talking about himself and how wonderful he is, never asking much about me. We ordered sushi and he made it apparent his was not for sharing. I've never had sushi where we didn't all share what was on the table? He continued to be a jerk to our waitress and mocked her niceness. Strike #4. I left to use the bathroom and wanted to make a dash for it, but he starred at me the whole walk back to the table. I gobbled down my sushi as quickly as possibly even though just listening to this guy made me nauseous. The entire date wasn't even hour, but I couldn't believe I wasted that much of my life with such a jerk. Those minutes of my life I'll never get back, though the sushi was delicious.

Listen to your Date

When going out on first dates it's important to *listen* to your date. Sometimes this is easier said than done, especially if you are a nervous talker. You start getting anxiety and keep talking to cover it up, yet you actually are showing that you are nervous. If you find yourself doing this, stop, take a deep breath and listen.

It's great if you are a talker because this is how someone is going to get to know you. No one wants to be on a date with a bump on a log. I've heard this from many guys, that women will just sit there on a date and not say anything. Make sure you are also listening to find out about him. If he's a great listener and you talk the entire night away, he knows everything about you, but what do you know about him?

Stop talking and start asking questions, that's when you start learning about someone else. When you ask a question make sure to fully listen to their answer and not preoccupy yourself with what your response is going to be. Ask about items that will reveal qualities to see if they match what you want in a partner. The last time I went speed-dating I thought I would conduct an experiment to see how many men asked me what I did for a living without me volunteering the information. Only three out of eight guys did. I asked them plenty of questions about themselves and they were happy to tell me. However it's a two-sided street, not a one-way avenue in getting to know someone. When your date asks you a question, when you are done answering flip it back to them. See what their opinion or answer is to the question they just asked you. On the speed-dates I even paused in-between questions giving them an opportunity to jump in and most did not. I know everyone gets nervous dating, yet you need to freshen up your conversation skills. If you have only six minutes to make an impression on someone, talking only about yourself that entire time isn't going to get you far. I left the event thinking wow no one really cared much about me. Funny though, the next day when I received my matches six of them were interested in me.

The Golden Rule of Meet-n-Greets

Of course everyone knows the ago old "Golden Rule," which is treat others as you want to be treated. We should all practice this is in our daily lives, whether it be in a romantic, friendly, or business way. I created a new Golden Rule within the meet-n-greets of online dating. This rule is a little bit different than the historic rule, yet should be followed.

The Golden Rule for meet-n-greets is: if you don't feel a connection during your short encounter, do not continue onto a longer version of the date. The whole point of the short meetings is to get a feel for the person and to find out if this is someone who you want to spend more time with and get to know better. If it's really not clicking, or this person is rubbing you the wrong way, end it politely and go your separate ways. Sometimes this is difficult if one party is totally into the other party, yet the other party isn't into them. Rejection is never easy, but don't force yourself to hang out with someone if the feelings are not there. Especially if you are an attractive male/ female, you probably get lots of people hitting on you all the time. It's nice, feels good, yet you are not obligated to spend time with that person. Just thank them for the compliment and move on. Don't force yourself to spend time with someone if they don't make your engines roar. It's honestly not fair to either person. You will just be leading them on and giving them false hope of a relationship that you know will never exist. Be honest with them and yourself.

Funny Dating Story

I met a man I had been talking to from the internet for a short coffee meeting. As soon as I saw him walk into Starbucks, I knew I wasn't attracted to him. We got our coffees and sat down to chat. He was very touchy feely which I'm not a big fan of just meeting someone. Keep the paws to yourself until we get to know each other better. I couldn't really understand him. I didn't know if he had an accent or wasn't pronouncing his words properly. So it was hard to have a conversation. The only thing I could understand was that he lied on his profile. He stated he didn't have children under 18, which in fact he did, a daughter who's 11. He said he put that because he hasn't seen her in two years. I don't know which is worse, that fact that he lied or that he's not in his daughter's life.

He proceeded to tell me of his ex-wife and that he escaped from her and moved to Florida to start over and he has no contact with his daughter. Though, his ex-wife always has a way of finding him knowing where he's working, where he's living and what car he's driving. I was thinking, um well, that's because you owe her child support!

All kinds of bells were going off in my head. He asked me to dinner. I don't know if my growling stomach was tuning out the alarm bells or I was suffering from low blood sugar, but I agreed to have dinner. As soon as I sat down I regretted my decision. I wasn't following my golden rule and I paid the consequences.

When I tried talking about something he would cut me off and tell me I didn't know what I was talking about. That I wasn't doing the proper research, he was right and I had no idea what was going on. It didn't feel like a conversation, it felt like a competition. It was exhausting. Finally I just chose to be quiet, eat my food and just smile and nod my way through it.

As he walked me to my car, I clicked my doors unlocked for a quick escape. Instead he pulled me towards him and I cranked my neck back. He says, "What no kiss?" Since I was held hostage I knew my only way out was a quick peck. So I obliged and pulled away.

Never forget the golden rule. If you're not feeling it during the quick coffee date, have a plan to leave shortly thereafter. Don't continue it. Trust your gut instincts. Listen to the bells going off in your head. They're there for a reason. Don't rationalize them away.

You don't always have to do coffee for a meet-n-greet; some people don't like coffee. Anything that's quick, easy and inexpensive is good. If you're not into caffeine maybe go for ice-cream. If you're a health nut go to a Jamba Juice or smoothie place. Any place that's in public that's comfortable and quiet enough to be able to have a conversation and get to know one another. Remember this is just an initial wedding out process. Once you decide that you do like this person, and then it's time for the first date.

It depends upon you if you want to extend the meet-n-greet for a longer first date. Sometimes I like to have the initial first date a few days after the short meeting. I'm a people pleaser by fault and sometimes I have a hard time saying no. If I'm on a meet-n-greet and not sure if I'm liking the guy and he asks me to go to dinner afterwards, (the example above) my knee jerk response is yes. I'm definitely getting better at saying no, though if you are a people pleaser, too, it might be in your best interest to leave the initial meeting to process your feelings. Sometimes it's good to take a day to reflect on it. Do I really like this person? How did they make me feel? Was I happy after I left their presence or did they make me feel bad about myself? If people are verbally abusive, negative or manipulative, you need space away to realize it most of the time. It can be hard in the meat of the situation to see that someone does not have your best interest at hand.

From the Y Chromosome

1) When do you think you should take the online romance offline?

Nathan – 28 – Single: *"I want to get the girls number within the second or third email and start talking on the phone soon. On the first phone conversation you have to ask her out on a date otherwise you're going to lose her."*

Dan – 56 – in a LTR: *"I don't want to send endless emails. A few emails, phone conversation, and then meet in person so we can see if we have chemistry. "*

2) What do you prefer to do on a first date?

Nathan – 28 – Single: *"A lounge where there's alcohol, I get nervous on coffee dates and a drink loosens me up. I would go for coffee she didn't drink though. I don't like getting food on a first date because she is going to evaluate how I'm eating my food."*

Dan – 56 – in a LTR: *"I would prefer going out to have a drink but I'm not going to spend more than $50. I took a lady from Match.com on a first date. I picked her up from her place and we went to a restaurant. I ordered a beer and she ordered a wine, then she asked the waitress about the lobster special. I told her if she's going to order lobster then she's going to get herself a cab ride home! "*

Chris – 41 – Divorced: *"I'm more traditional so I'll take a date out to dinner and buy, it's no problem. I'm not expecting anything in return. If she orders lots of wine and gets drunk that's a bad sign. Or if she wants to go somewhere expensive I'm not doing that, but something like Outback is fine. Quick meetings are good too or doing something different like ice skating. Then if it goes well then ask them for ice cream afterwards."*

Jerry – 60 – in a LTR: *"I prefer coffee, a glass of wine or a light dinner. One time I was supposed to meet a lady for a glass of wine on our first date. I picked her up at her house, and at first glance she was not the same person in her photo. She was very large and wearing dress that was too short, her slip was showing the entire night. She kept complaining about life and was very negative. We went to Armani's whish is a very high class restaurant because she wanted to watch the sunset over the water. I didn't have a problem with that, yet when we got there she made reservations for us for dinner. That wasn't our plan, yet since I'm a gentleman I had dinner with her. Nonetheless she couldn't even hold a conversation. I kept asking things about her and I would get one word responses. The bill came and it was $150 for dinner, I of course paid for it. Yet she still looked miserable and at the end she wanted to go out again. I told her I didn't think we were a match, but I always try to leave on a positive note."*

OVERVIEW: Rule # 5

- Meet your online romance in the flesh within two weeks.
- When you do meet, go somewhere public; never have a first date pick you up from your house.
- Use short meet-n-greets as short, 30 minute coffee dates.
- If you're not feeling chemistry, don't extend the meet-n-greet onto dinner.

RULE #6
BE SAFE RESEARCH YOUR DATE

This is a rule that is also in my previous book, "10 Rules to Survive the Dating Jungle." I have it in this book as well because it is a very important rule, especially when it comes to dating. But it's something we can and should do with everything in our lives. For example, business dealings, baby sitters, just about anyone!

Protecting Yourself and Your Information

In this day and age of meeting people over the internet through chat rooms and various other methods, you need to make sure to be safe. Even if you met a guy/girl in person at a bar, you never know who they really are. When you set up dates, make sure to both drive your own car and meet somewhere public. Tell one of your friends where you are going and the name of your date. Never meet anyone at their house or yours. You don't want them knowing where you live just in case the date goes bad and you never want to see them again. It's best to keep meeting in public places until the third date or so, just to make sure you think you know the other person satisfyingly enough to let them come and pick you up.

When meeting someone online, don't give out your phone number right away. If someone asks for your phone number after a few conversations, give them your email address first. I would recommend creating an email that you will use just for dating purposes. Do not give out your work email because: (a) it's not professional and (b) that person will know exactly where you work. These are not smart things to do with someone you do not know very well. If things go wrong, they may start stalking you at your work. (Example: I dated a guy for a month or so and he had my work email. When I decided he wasn't the one for me, he got very upset and subscribed my work email to all kinds of pornographic websites. I was bombarded during the day with thousands of nasty emails. I finally had to tell my boss, and the company had to delete that email account and create me an entirely new one-- not particularly a fun thing to happen at work!)

Don't give out a personal email that you use for Facebook, forums, or any other online websites either. If you Google the email address you use to log into Facebook, your Facebook page will pull up in the search engine results. If you do not have your Facebook profile set to private, this person will be able to see all your photos, all your friends and family members, and any other important information you have on there. God forbid you have your home address listed. BAM! This stranger now knows exactly where you live. The amount of information a complete stranger can pull up on you is kind of scary. You have to be internet-smart. If you do use social media I suggest making your pages private. Facebook tends to change its privacy settings frequently, so make sure to keep it up to date The best thing to do is create a Yahoo! or Gmail account to be used strictly for dating purposes. When creating this account, use your real first name, but do not put your entire last name. For example, I would name mine *Tara R.* That way when you email them, they will not know exactly what your last name is so they can't search you by full name either. They will find out your full name in time, if they prove themselves worthy.

Sometimes people you chat with on dating sites will ask you if you have a Facebook or MySpace. They want to add you as a friend so they can find out more information about you. DO NOT ADD ANYONE YOU DON'T KNOW ON SOCIAL MEDIA SITES! I cannot emphasize this enough.

You never know who people are: who's fake, who's creepy and who's stalking you. For one thing, if you add someone you don't know on Facebook and do the "check in" feature at an establishment, they know where you are all the time. They might just pop up unexpected. Then they have access to your friend list and can find out all kinds of information about you. It also makes it very difficult in the early stages of dating if you're still in the weeding out process and casually dating other people.

For example: a guy asks you out on a Friday night but you already have a date planned. You arrange to see him Saturday and he's on your Facebook page. Your friends comment on your page to ask how your hot date went, and Mr. Saturday sees it. Obviously everyone is just dating until you have the "commitment conversation," but who knows, your next date may be a little mentally unstable. He may freak out that you went out with someone else. It's fine to date until you are monogamous with someone, but others usually don't want you shoving it in their face. You should be a little bit coyer about it.

Finding out if Your Date is Safe

Making sure that your potential date is not a serial killer might seem a little overboard, but in this day and age, it's better to be safe than sorry. You know how easy it is to find information on someone over the internet, so utilize it. There are lots of free resources online, depending on what counties you live in, just Google certain items. In most counties you can search criminal files and the jail databases. It's all public information to find out who's in jail and what crime they are being held for. Most databases will be able to tell you the arrest record on a certain individual for up to 15 years online for free. It will list their name, date of birth, crime, and mug shot so you know if it's the same person. You can also search for registered sex offenders. All sex offenders must register wherever they live and you can even search by someone's email address. Of course, email addresses are easy to create, but it doesn't hurt to try. Since you can't necessarily ask someone for their social or driver's license number, use all the info you can. Even just Googling someone's name brings up a plethora of information. Just make sure it's on the right person. There are lots of similar names out there.

For example, if you wanted to search criminal records for Hillsborough County in Tampa, you would Google "Hillsborough County Sheriff Dept." Click "Arrest Inquiry" and it presents a search box. All you have to enter is last name, first name, race, and sex, then you'll be given the arrest records. Most searches go a few years back. Hillsborough Sheriff's office has records online for 16 years. You may have to search multiple counties if you live somewhere where there are a lot of adjacent areas. If you know your date has just moved from a different area, get the name of the county or state and search there as well. Don't be too obvious, like asking, "Oh, what was the name of the county you lived in?" Just find out the city and remember it, then you can Google it the next day to find out what county it is. Most county-level searches are free.

If you want to do a statewide criminal search, depending on your state's laws, you may have to pay for it. Make sure you have the most accurate information on the person you want to search: full name, birthdate, race, sex, height, weight, eye color, and hair color. You do not want to pay for inaccurate records. You can do the statewide criminal searches through government websites as well. I trust these over other sites that basically pull the same information but might cost you more. Arrest records are public in most states, though some people can order to have their records sealed or expunged. This means that you would not be able to find their records even if they had been arrested or convicted of a crime. Keep in mind that even if no records come back in these searches, they will still charge you the fees.

The National Sex Offender database (http://www.familywatchdog.us) is free, and you can search by state or name. You can also search the entire US for the same name. This is helpful for more than just dating purposes. If you have children, it helps keep track of sex offenders who move into your neighborhood.

If you want to find out if someone is married, divorced, or has other domestic records, that can be found in your county's Clerk of Court office. All this is public information as well. Each county is different with their process for searching records. Most counties should have a searchable database online. Just Google "Clerk of Court Records (your county)." For example, Hillsborough County records go back to 1965; that's a pretty decent time frame. Sometimes in the search field it works best to just use the last name. Most marriage and divorce records have the person's middle name recorded, so if you don't know their entire name and search by just the first and last name, it may not pull up anything. Just search by the person's last name and you will get more results to filter through. Now remember, if you are searching for women within the marriage documents, the marriage certificate will show up under her maiden name. Just keep that into consideration. For men it's easier, since they do not change their last name.

Be wary of those online background checks that promote finding information only from someone's name. There are a lot of people with the same name out there. I've already done searches on myself and there's way more Tara Richters out there in the world than I would have hoped for! You need to make sure you are getting the correct information on the correct person. You don't want to pay $100 only to find random information on the wrong person. It's better to be more specific, such as the county of residence or birth date, so you can narrow it down. Don't go too crazy either. Just do a few checks to make sure this person is who they say they are. If you start getting the feeling that something wishy-washy is going on, you're probably right. Trust your instincts.

Just Googling someone's name can pull up a vast array of items. LinkedIn.com and CorporationWiki.com is an easy way to find out someone's executive profiles to see if they really do have the job or work for the company they say they do. Just doing simple checks like to see if their stories jive is never a bad idea. Just do keep in mind, like I said before, there are people out there with the same name. For example, if I Google Tara Richter, I apparently am a photographer for Richter Photography, a graduate of Hononegah High School in Rockton, IL, a teacher in Greenville County, and also a graduate of Richland Center High School in Richland Center, WI. This is all on the first page of results. None of those are actually me.

How to Find out if Someone you Met Online is Married

Unfortunately, this happens quit often in the online dating scene. Men and woman are out there prowling around the internet looking for something on the side, and others are trying to test the waters to see if they should leave their marriage (some are out right honest about it). When I was a member of Plenty of Fish, a guy emailed me about meeting for drinks. When I checked his profile, because I always do prior to responding, it flat out stated he was married, had been contemplating cheating on his wife and now was the time. His headline stated "Don't judge me." He even posted a photo! That's pretty ballsy considering everyone I know within the Tampa Bay area and is single is pretty much on this site. This man made it very easy to decide if you wanted to help him commit infidelity; usually this isn't the case.

Since I was cheated on during the three major relationships in my life (first fiancé, second fiancé and then eventually my husband), I believe myself to be an expert on this topic. I have been the wife/ fiancée witnessing the weird behaviors from the supposedly committed man and also ended up being the other woman without my previous knowledge. There are signs to tell if the person you are talking to on the internet is married or already in a committed relationship based on behaviors I have witnessed:

They don't have a photo on their profile. This is just obvious. I never respond or contact anyone on a dating website who doesn't have a photo. In this day and age everyone has a digital photo. Either you have one via smart phone, camera, web cam, or someone else has one of these devices to take one for you. Don't believe the lies that they don't know how. Really? Do you even want to date someone that stupid; who doesn't know how to upload a photo to the internet? Even my 67 year old father can take photos and upload them to an email. If they don't have a photo they are either: a) concealing their identity because they are in a committed relationship or b) butt-ass ugly.

They only email you and will not give out their phone number. One man who I discovered was married from researching him (in the example story below), wouldn't give me his phone number. He would only email me, yet wanted to meet me an hour away in Orlando. If you're going to meet someone in person you need to get their digits just in case you end up at the wrong place. If they are reluctant, it's because they don't want you calling them and their wife/ husband answering the phone.

They give you their phone number, but only call during working hours and disappear after 6 or 7 p.m. This little trick I discovered from my ex-husband and I'll thank him for that. He started dating an old high school sweet heart via Facebook during our marriage. She got suspicious that he would only call and talk to her during the daytime, while he was in the office, or in his car on his way home from work. After 6 p.m. every night he would go MIA (missing in action). He wouldn't return her text messages or phone calls. Why? Because he was in our home eating dinner with me, his wife. Be very suspicious if the person you are dating is only available certain hours of the day.

They will only meet you in secluded places off the beaten path. Say you want to meet your date at the new posh place for dinner and they instead suggest a small restaurant way off the freeway out in the middle of nowhere; there's something up. They obviously don't want to be seen out in public with you. If you live in the same area of town, they most likely are married, so they can't risk taking you to a popular place because a friend, coworker or relative might see you two together. Sometimes quaint places are a nice change of pace, yet if it happens a lot take a step back and reevaluate your situation.

They are never available around the holidays. If you've been dating someone for a while, but they can never hang out with you during, say, New Year's Eve, Halloween, Valentine's Day, etc. It's most likely because they're spending that quality time with their family. I don't mean mom and dad; I mean their wife and kids.

Let's say that you invite your new boyfriend to your friends costume party that happens to fall right on Halloween; he says he has to work late and can't go. He could be lying and really has to take his kids out trick-or-treating. Or this classic move, which I have to give credit to my second fiancé for, he says he has to work on Valentine's Day night. He takes me out to dinner the night prior instead. He wasn't really working; he was just trying to fit two different dates in on one holiday. Someone else got the Valentine's Day date; I, instead, got shafted with the day before. Of course sometimes people do have to work and schedules may conflict, though if you start seeing a pattern, be suspicious.

Utilize these helpful hints if you think there might be something suspicious with a person you're chatting with online or have just started dating. The one thing you can always turn to when you have questions is your gut. Trust yourself and your intuitions. I never did in my twenties and it lead me to two failed engagements and a nasty divorce. My gut was always right, but my head told me to believe the lies my significant other was feeding me. Never let anyone instill doubt within yourself. You're smart and you know what's best for you. If you can't trust yourself then who can you trust?

Funny Dating Story

I met a guy on a dating website. We conversed through email and a few text messages for about a week. His profile said he lived in Orlando, but when I asked, he said he didn't really have a place he called home. He traveled all the time for work. Though he used to live in Illinois, goes to London for work, but right now is living out of hotel rooms. That sounded a little fishy, but I know some people travel a lot for business. He said he was a coach, mentor and does speaking engagements. He wanted me to come up to Orlando for a date and said he wanted to take me shopping at the outlet mall. Well, what girl would turn that down? So we planned on a date for the following week. He canceled a few days later and said he had to go back to London to fill in for a friend at the last minute. I asked what he did in London for work; he said he takes people to watch soccer games. That sounded weird to me too. Why do you need to take them to watch soccer? Can't they just go themselves? He wanted to reschedule our date for the following week.

I decided to do some research on this guy. Before I drove all the way to Orlando and back (which would be a three hour round trip) I needed to find out more details. He had not given me a lot of info about him; he was always asking questions about me. He asked me if I was married; I told him I was divorced, yet I asked him the same and he didn't respond. Instead, he changed the subject. Also, he would never call me. It's easier for him to text in front of his wife versus calling.

I had his full name and business email address. I Googled it and I found his LinkedIn.com profile. On his profile it had his personal and business websites. I went to those and discovered he had opened a Great Clips. It had photos of him, a woman and a child. So, I assumed he's married with a child. It had her name, Lisa, within the captions of the photos, but nothing more. I went back to LinkedIn.com and his profile stated that his business served the greater Chicago, Illinois area. I went to WhitePages.com and searched him in Chicago. It actually pulled up that he lived right outside in a small town in Wisconsin. Though, on WhitePages.com it will tell you the address, who else is living in that household and their approximate age range. The name of the woman in the photos matched the information on WhitePages.com. I wanted to see if I could pull up their marriage certificate, even though for me this was evidence enough that he was a married man. I searched their address to find the county they resided in. It came up as Kenosah. I went to the Kenosah County Clerk of Courts website. Unfortunately, Kenosah makes you pay to search family records. I didn't want to cough up the money, so instead I searched the Kenosah Circuit Court Records. I discovered that their house went into foreclosure at the beginning of year with his wife's name on the docket. Also, he was sued for an automobile/injury accident back in 1993. Right there, the proof is in the pudding. I found out he's married without needing to search the family courts. If her name is on the foreclosure docket, then it had to have been on the title, mortgage and/or deed. Normally, you wouldn't have someone on title, etc. unless it's a spouse or in other cases a sibling/parent. I didn't believe the latter to be the case, especially since I saw their family portrait on the Great Clips website.

I decided I would let this man know that I discovered he was married. I didn't want to send an email asking if he was because he could say things like "oh we're separated," and yadda yadda. I wanted him to know that I knew everything about him without threatening him, just to make him shake in his boots a little. I sent him a short email; all it said was, "So, how is Lisa doing?" I never heard back.

Within 15 minutes I discovered all this information on a man I was conversing with over the internet. Thank goodness for public records! It's so easy in this day and age to find out if someone is full of crap or telling you the truth. The internet is a great tool to find information and most of it is for FREE. You need to take responsibility for who you are dating. Don't leave it up to them. You don't want to get involved in a relationship and then two months down the line have some woman come knocking on your door. It's just like defensive driving. It would be nice to think everyone's a good driver, but they're not. The roads are filled with crazy drivers that do stupid things like pull out in front of you. You have to slam on your breaks and swerve out of the way to avoid getting your car smashed. The same goes for dating; practice safe dating. Be smart, do your research, it will save you a lot of grief down the road!

Another Real World Experience for Business Purposes

This detective story is going a little bit off the dating path, but it still demonstrates how doing your research saves your butt in the long run. Along with being an author, I'm also a real estate agent, as you know from reading my first chapter. I had a tenant living in my house (the one I had while I was married and then rented when we got divorced). The previous tenants broke their lease and left me high and dry to find new tenants to occupy the property.

Since this is 2012 and the real estate market is not good, it's difficult to buy, sell, or rent any real estate. Plus my house is 5 bedrooms, 3 baths; it's very large so I need a decent amount of rent to pay the mortgage, taxes and HOA. It was grueling trying to get any appointments to show it. Finally I made one with a single mother of three, though two were over 18 years old. She told me over the phone that her current landlord was getting his house taken back from the bank and she was getting kicked out and needed something by the 1st of the month. I sympathized with her situation and we scheduled the appointment.

I met with her the following day, which was about a week prior to the first of the month. She loved the house and, even though she had three kids, only one was going to be occupying the house with her. I thought that was a lot of room for two people, but if she wants it, who am I to judge? So she took an application and said she would get it over to me soon for the background check.

That same night, she said she really wanted the house and she would get me the application to me soon. I said I would run her information and get back to her. Two days passed and nothing came into my email. I finally emailed her and asked if she had sent it. She responded that she couldn't figure out how to scan and email it. I told her it wasn't a problem and that she could fax it instead. I went ahead and created an e-fax account so she could fax it to me. Two days later, there was still no fax.

By this point, I was really irritated. I emailed her stating that I needed the application and the deposit of $2,100 in order to save the property for her and that I had other prospective tenants interested. I finally received a phone call a full 24 hours after that email. Hurricane Isaac had come through the Tampa Bay area that weekend, yet we had minimal winds and rain. All the locals actually made jokes about it because we really missed everything. But she claimed that the storm broke her window and the rain damaged her iPhone and laptop at the same time so she was just now getting her stuff in order. By this time I was calling bullshit on everything that was coming out of her mouth. It seemed she was trying to hide something. I still gave her the benefit of the doubt. She claimed she was opening a restaurant and was very busy. That raised another red flag because it seemed odd that a single mother could afford $4,200 for a deposit/ first months rent and be opening a restaurant, though who knows, maybe a rich uncle died?

Finally, almost a week after the fact, she still could not get the application to me. Even though she was supposedly opening a business, she couldn't figure out how to fax, scan, email or mail something through the post office. So irritated by this point, I told her to give me her name, social and date of birth, which she did. I ran the background check from a software I have a membership to and everything came back fine. My intuition, on the other hand, was not fine. I just knew I smelled a rat.

So I started doing my own searches. I searched the name and date of birth in both Hillsborough and Pinellas county websites. Nothing pulled up, but her email address had a different name embedded in it. I tried those two together and nothing. Then I remembered she told me the name of her restaurant she was opening. I went to sunbiz.org, which is where all businesses in the state of Florida must be registered. That did pull up and even stated that it had been dissolved two years prior. So a) that means she lied to me about opening a restaurant, and b) it had her REAL FULL name listed as the owner. Once I had that information along with her birthday all the worms came out of the can.

In Hillsborough County, she had been arrested 13 times from 1995 to 2012. Most of the arrests had multiple charges that varied from check fraud for property gain to grand theft auto and seven counts of Uttering a Forged Instrument. The latter is when you forge a financial document such as a deed. I lost track of how many check frauds there were to gain property. So I'm assuming she wrote bad checks, gained a property, and then moved when it bounced (it takes about 90 days to legally remove someone from the property). I think this is how she was keeping a roof over her head. I was so shocked, yet happy that I finally discovered the truth. It wasn't that hard, yet I had to do some deep digging since she gave me three aliases, one of which was misspelled.

If you are smart and use your free online resources, you can discover a lot about someone, even if they do give you fake information. The nice thing about the police departments is that you can search by just first name, last name, sex, race or birthdate. It may take longer, but it's well worth it in the long run. Always trust your gut instinct, too. Even though my background software came back with OK on everything, I knew something was fishy. All the pieces just didn't add up. She was super sweet on the phone, in person and kept trying to manipulate me with her sob stories. I didn't buy it. When I confronted her with what I discovered, she then made a play that she was a victim of identity theft. I didn't buy that either. All 13 mug shots looked just like her. Sorry, you can't get anything by me.

Don't fall fool to other peoples' games and sympathy cards. So many others will manipulate and try to play you to gain access to anything they need from you. Within business and in the dating world, don't fall for it. Trust yourself and trust your gut. There are lots of men and women who will try to play your heart to get into your wallet and rip you off. If you think someone is trying to scam you, they probably are. Be smart, do your research and become your own detective.

From the Y Chromosome

1) Was there any woman you met online you felt unsafe about?

Dan – 56 – In a LTR: "*I met a woman on Match.com. She contacted me and said she was going through a divorce. She made a lot of money and was a nice lady, though we went three times and on the third date had sex. I didn't feel chemistry, she kept keep calling and I didn't want to talk to her because it just wasn't the right sexual chemistry. That's a big thing! Plus I found out her ex was still living in her house.*"

Jerry – 60 – in a LTR: "*On millionaire match.com I emailed a women that had a very well written profile with a beautiful picture. However, I thought I maybe too old for her. So I just sent a nice email to compliment her. She responded with just her phone number. I called her and we had a nice conversation. She said that she was an attorney which I found interesting since I was as well. We would call or chat over instant messaging for a while. Then for no reason she started asking obscure questions, like strange things about my driving record. Consequently I started doing research on her. I went online to The State Bar Examination website to find her license, yet her name did not pull up. When I confronted her she said she practices law under a different name. Everything kept getting weirder and weirder, and she's obviously misrepresenting herself. She kept sending photos but all of them a little blurry and didn't necessarily look all like the same person. When I implied I wasn't sure she was being honest, she responds that she'll have to fly down and visit to prove it. She lived in Atlanta and purchased a flight down to Florida. I made reservations at a hotel but she wouldn't give me her flight itinerary or arrival time. She said she would call me when she arrived. I never received a phone call, she never showed up, I really didn't think she would. Yet it irritated me, why was she just jerking me around? I emailed her and ask why she was wasting my time? She*" responded with, 'grow up loser'. Then two weeks later she sends me an IM and wants to meet again. I retorted the Latin phrase that all attorneys know, 'Res ipsa loquitur' (it speaks for itself). She had no idea what I was referring to."

2) Do you think men should do background checks on women they meet online?

Nathan – 28 – Single: "*Good precaution but I've never done one. You just have to ask about their relationship history. One lady I went out with said she had to file restraining orders on a few guys she met online. That was kind of strange, but I continued to go out with her another three or four times.*"

3) How do you feel if a woman ran a background check on you prior to a first date?

Nathan – 28 – Single: "*I wouldn't care.*"

Dan – 56 – In a LTR: "*It wouldn't bother me.*"

Chris – 41 – Divorced: "*That's fine, however there's a guy that lives in Virginia with my exact same name that has a record. So if women tell me they're going to search me I'll let them know that in advance.*"

Jerry – 60 – in a LTR: "*I have no problem with it, if they have any discern with me, I have nothing to hide.*"

4) Have you ever discovered a woman lied in her profile, if so did you confront her about it?

Nathan – 28 – Single: "*One chick said she smoked pot in person, which she marked no on her profile. I didn't say anything, but I didn't go out with her again.*"

Dan – 56 – In a LTR: "*Yea, I have. If it's just their age a few years or so that's not a big deal. Yet if she was fat in person and said she was skinny in her profile that is not cool.*"

Jerry – 60 – in a LTR: *"Most women I have found have misrepresented their weight/ body size. Some will lie about their age a few years and that's not a big deal. I never confronted them about it because I'm not confrontational. I just tell them after the date that there just wasn't any chemistry there. I always do a follow up email either way after a date to have closure. "*

5) Have you ever come across women trying to scam you on websites?

Nathan – 28 – Single: *"Twice I have, both were from singlesnet.com. One was from Russia and said she needed a plane ticket. The other one said she was traveling abroad and lost her wallet."*

Dan – 56 – In a LTR: "*No.****"*

Chris – 41 – Divorced: "*No scammers, but fake profiles where they said in their bio they have big blue eyes and in the photo their eyes were green."*

Jerry – 60 – in a LTR: *"I receive messages on Yahoo IM from scammers. One girl who said she's going to a university in Russia. The photo of her was superhot. I played with it to see where she was going to take it. She would write long nice letters. Always sent photos along with them, they were all very pretty so I liked looking .I told her I will never send money. She freaked out and said, 'How dare you accuse me of something like that!' Then a few weeks later she told me she was coming to the states and was $200 short. I told her I wouldn't send money, I never heard from her again."*

OVERVIEW: Rule #6

- Keep your personal information private in the beginning.
- Don't add dates on Facebook until you really get to know them.
- Do you research and Google dates, don't just believe what they tell you.
- Most importantly listen to your gut instincts, they're always right.

RULE #7
IS THIS THE ONE FOR ME?

You've done your weeding out process online, you've narrowed it down to a few coffee meet-n-greets and now *finally* one person shines out from the rest. Your online profile starts to gather dust as you spend more time concentrating on this one person and finding out if they are the right one for you. If everything seems great, just take your time to see how they are in different situations. Everyone can put on their best behavior in the beginning; the true test is when difficult times and chaos arise, those will show someone's true colors.

Remember to keep your head on straight and your feet on the ground! It's easy to get caught up in a fantasy, but most of the time those stories end in sadness, because that's what they are, just stories, not reality. If a guy or girl seems too good to be true, that may just be the case; they could be lying. I'm not saying every great date you had was a liar, but just keep an eye out. Time will tell with everyone. You want someone who can withstand the test of time and who can grow old with you, so don't get too anxious and leech onto the next person you have a date with.

Be happy with yourself. Know deep down inside that you will be virtuous and survive no matter who comes in or out of your life. When you're secure within yourself you will glow with that self-confidence which attracts other healthy people. Being insecure and needy is just going to attract the guy or girl who wants to take advantage of someone's insecurities. Don't settle for less; you deserve a loving, wonderful person who will treat you and love you 100 percent!

Third Date Rule

If you've been out on three dates with the same person and you're just not sure if you're feeling it, move on. It shouldn't take that long to discover if you're attracted to someone or not. Sure they maybe witty, charming, nice, sweet, yet if you're just not convinced they're the one for you, move on. There's no point in continuing to date someone if the chemistry isn't there. They may be the sweetest guy in the world or the nicest girl, but if it doesn't get your engines going by now it probably won't ever. Don't get stuck with someone where you don't think there's long term potential. Some people stay in relationships because there's nothing better to do. If it's not fulfilling to you, get out and find someone who is.

Don't try so hard to make it work. The more time you spend with Mr./Mrs. Wrong is the less time you have to find Mr./Mrs. Right. After three dates neither party should be too emotionally invested. It's easier to break it off now versus dragging it out longer and breaking hearts. If you're not sure by date three, be polite and let them know they're just not the one for you. You should be fully into someone to keep dating them. Be courteous and hopefully you can still gain a friendship from it. Never burn bridges or drag it out to the point where you just can't stand the site of the other person.

Even if the guy/girl is totally into you, make sure the feeling is mutual. You don't have to stay in a relationship just to please them. I'm sure they'll be a little bit sad, but more grateful if you're up front and honest with them. I really think people value truth. Just make sure you can be honest with yourself. If you are an attractive person you can have many people pursue you, just because they are doesn't mean you have to date all of them. Hold out for the one who makes you just as happy as you make them.

He/ She is so Nice, But...

I've heard the beginning of this statement so many times by so many girlfriends and it has even come out of my mouth: "He's so nice, but.... he cheated, he lied, he has a girlfriend in another state, he's not divorced yet, he makes me feel bad." Then he's NOT a nice guy! We have to stop brain washing ourselves and thinking that everyone is nice. If his actions show him as inconsiderate, rude or mean then he is not a nice guy.

If we look up the definition of "nice" in the dictionary it states:
adjective nic•er, nic•est.
1. pleasing; agreeable; delightful: a nice visit.
2. amiably pleasant; kind: They are always nice to strangers.
3. characterized by, showing, or requiring great accuracy, precision, skill, tact, care, or delicacy: nice workmanship; a nice shot; a nice handling of a crisis.

Nowhere does it state nice as someone who manipulates, lies or cheats in the above definition. We need to stop making excuses and start being honest with ourselves and not giving anyone the benefit of the doubt until they prove themselves worthy.

One of my girlfriends met a guy on Match.com and went out with him a few times. He "seemed" like a nice guy, I even met him on the 4th of July. Then she tells me one night that he has a girlfriend back in Michigan and he hasn't told her he's dating other people yet. His girlfriend was supposed to move down to Florida, but hasn't. He gave her a deadline that she needed to move by or he was breaking up with her. My mouth dropped open as I was assuming the next words from my friend would go something like this, "So then I dumped him and said I wasn't going to play second fiddle."

Instead she went on with the "nice guy" introduction. I protested back that he was not a nice guy. Why would anyone want to play second fiddle and wait around to see if this guy's girlfriend will show up in a few weeks? He's being dishonest with his current girlfriend, so why would he be honest with my friend? His tarnished character was showing already and she had only been on a few dates with him. Time to kick him to the curb, which she did finally. A few months after, she discovered his girlfriend decided to make the move and they had a shot gun wedding. He went from meeting my girlfriend on Match.com to marrying another women in all of five months!

If someone is not going to make you their top priority and give you 100 percent, why would you waste your time? It's definitely not fair to invest your heart and soul into someone and get only 25 percent back in return. You would be upset with your bank if you deposited $1,000 into your checking account and next month when you went to withdraw it there was only $250 left. Heads would roll, managers would be called, letters written to newspapers, and everyone would know! Why is it when the same thing happens in relationships we let them get by with it? We keep giving and they keep withdrawing without ever making a deposit and we just say, "Oh he's a nice guy, but he's just too busy to go out with me on my birthday." Invest in yourself and only partner with someone who will increase your stock

Dating Tests

When you first start dating someone, you may or may not realize you are putting that person through a series of tests. Sometimes they are planned tests or they may be subconscious. Either way, it's good to see how this person reacts within different situations. Obviously, it takes a long time to really get to know a person, but you can try to speed up the process a little bit. Here are a few tests I have done with gents that might be potential relationship material to see if he can go the distance:

1)The Mall Test – For a first shopping excursion, you might want to keep it short and sweet. You don't want to completely torture the guy. Ease him in by stopping by a sports-related store first. Or lure him there by doing what I did with a guy I was dating and say you want to go pick out a Red Sox shirt and you want his opinion. Of course, use some team he follows. Obviously, don't say you want to buy a Red Sox shirt if he's a Yankees fan. You might just end the relationship right then and there! Do some research first. After you browse the sports gear, take him over to Macy's, NYCO or another department store. See how long he can stand watching you pick out clothes and trying stuff on. Does he get agitated easily or is he happy to hold your purse for you? Hold up a garment that's truly awful and ask his opinion. Does he lie and say it's wonderful or is he honest with you? If you're going to be in a long-term relationship with someone you each are going to have to compromise your time and do things that may not be on your top of the list of fun stuff to do. Make sure he's at least willing to be a good sport for you.

2)The Alcohol Test – This one you probably want to wait until you know the other person fairly well. I'm not talking about getting totally smashed and blacking out around your date. You really don't even have to drink that much. You can pretend you're a little tipsier than you really are. Act a little foolish, do something kind of stupid in public and see how he reacts. Is he completely embarrassed and ridicule you like a child? Or does he take care of you like a gentleman should? Not everyone is perfect all the time. There may be times when you're sick, emotional or a little tipsy. You want to know that this guy has your back. Marriage isn't puppy dog tails and butterflies 24-7. You don't want a guy who's only going to be around you when you are perfectly proper.

On my last birthday while I was with my ex-husband, I had a little too much wine and was having a little too much fun with my friends. He got upset and said I was making a mockery of him. I got upset and starting crying. His way of dealing with it was to basically throw me outside of the club, put me on a bench and leave me there all by myself. I was so upset and crying so hard slouched over on the iron rod bench, which was already on a tilt, and it flipped over and fell on top of me. It was embarrassing, to say the least, and it left a big nasty bruise on my thigh for a month. He obviously didn't win husband of the year.

3)The Friend Test – I think pretty much everyone does the friend test. I wouldn't do this one right away either. I want to make sure I've had enough time to get to know this person before I introduce them to my friends. If you don't take time to be alone with your date first to make sure there's a connection, your friends can cloud your judgment. I would say go on at least five or six dates prior to them meeting your friends. I don't advise bringing friends along on first dates either. It makes for a really awkward situation. They're not going to get your group's inner jokes and are going to feel left out. Once you decide you do like this person and want to introduce them to your friends, start with a small group setting as to not overwhelm them. See how he treats your friends. Is he talkative, nice, and social? Or does he try to flirt with your girlfriends? Don't have a blind eye to mischievous behavior. I had this scenario happen with a girlfriend and myself. Every time I hung out with her and her boyfriend, she would get really tipsy and her boyfriend would hit on me. It made me very uncomfortable and she never realized it even though it was happening right in front of her! It got to the point where he got my phone number and started texting me asking me out. At that point I had hard core evidence and showed it to her. You can't argue with a text message. This guy was obviously a douche.

4)The Pet Test – Animals have great instincts. They can sniff out a jerk and can also sense a caring person. If you have a dog, cat or other furry friend, bring your date home sometime and introduce them to Fido or Fluffy. Watch how he interacts with them. Does he screech and runaway? Or does get down on his knees and play with him? I personally have a cat and she does not like men much. Though, it's funny because she'll be nice to some men and not to others. I've even noticed she'll get snippy with some of my girlfriends that turned out to be not-so-nice people. Animals can tell. If your pet really doesn't like a certain person, the animal's instincts are probably right. Plus, I love my cat. I've had her for three years now after adopting her from the humane society. They said when she was four months old she had feline leukemia. I adopted her anyway and three years later she's leukemia free. If someone doesn't get along with my cat, well I'm sorry, I choose Callie over him.

These are just a few examples of tests to see if your potential date can go the distance with you. There are many more small tests you want to implement throughout the relationship process.

Does Your Date Drive You to Drink?

Do you ever notice that being around certain people drives you to drink? Of course we all have relatives and friends that make us want to drink in order to be around them. Especially around the holidays, which thank goodness at those occasions it's usually acceptable to crack open a bottle of wine at 11 AM. If it wasn't we may have more violence at the table than just slicing the turkey.

Since being back in the dating jungle, I've noticed certain guys I go out on dates with I only have fun if I am drinking alcohol. That's why I made my first date rule to have coffee dates instead of happy hour. Though, sometimes they pass the first few sober dates test. Then a few weeks into it, I find myself always going for the wine when I'm in their presence.

I dated a man from POF for a about a month who was super nice and sweet, but rather annoying in his personality. He just did things that got under my skin. I'm very organized and detail oriented and he lived more in his head, up above in the clouds somewhere.

I realized the only way I could relax and enjoy being around him was, well, if I had a decent buzz. If I was sober I wanted to drop kick his ass out the car. Obviously, once coming to this conclusion I had to break it off. If you have to be inebriated in order to tolerate someone, it's not going to work out in the long haul.

We may not even realize that we are drinking in order to impair our own judgment just to be with someone. We tell ourselves consciously that this is a good person for us, that we should be with them. Though, if it's just not clicking and you can't stand to be around that person, it doesn't matter how nice they are. Don't impair your judgment just to tolerate someone.

It can go the other way, too, where your boyfriend / girlfriend may do disrespectful things in your presence such as hitting on all your friends or strangers when you two are out together. So in order to avoid the situation and not confront the issue head on, you start drinking to ignore it. Obviously this doesn't work. It just makes the problem worse. If you can't enjoy the company of your partner fully sober, then it may be time to find someone new.

Misinterpreting Signals

That slight touch of the hand or arm around your shoulder from the opposite sex may not necessarily be a signal they are into you. Some people are just more touchy feely than others. Alcohol may also come

118

into play. Are they really into you or are they just more flirty and at ease with a few cocktails in their system?

One of my clients told me over the phone that a woman kept squeezing his shoulder, so that definitely means she was into him. No, it doesn't. Just because a man or woman gives you a hug or squeezes your shoulder doesn't mean anything. They're showing affection, yet not necessarily giving you a signal they want to jump into bed. Signals can be misinterpreted. Be sure you are the reading the other person correctly or it can be embarrassing for both parties.

It can also be a cultural thing. In some countries you don't shake hands, you embrace, others kiss on the cheek and some bow. If a lady approached you and grabbed your junk or a man went for your breasts, that probably means they want you... in the sack... now. Unless they are from a part of the world I'm unfamiliar with and this is normal interaction.

If someone grazes your arm or does something you think is more intentional than a friendly hello, watch for other signals. After they brushed by you are they now flirting with you from across the way? Do they keep making eye contact? Or do they have their back turned towards you? It may have been accidental.

Studies say that a man subconsciously points his groin area in the direction of the woman he's most into. He may have his face directed to the person he's speaking with, yet his body is facing you. If he is really interested, eventually he will speak to you so his whole body is focused on what he wants most. If a woman is interested she coyly flips her hair back and forth and every now and then looks in the direction of her desire. Not for too long though, then quickly looks away.

If instead your playmate ventures off to talk to someone else and stops looking at you, then maybe she lost interest or you misinterpreted the signals. Would you stop talking to someone you were interested in? Maybe only if you got interrupted, but you would eventually go back if you indeed were intrigued. You're like a bug being pulled into the light, you can't control it. Though, if you misinterpret the signals you may end up getting zapped!

Signs of Controlling Behavior

Recognizing the early signs of controlling behavior in a partner can be more difficult if you grew up in a household with controlling parents. During your childhood if whoever raised you was very controlling and manipulative it's a behavior that you are used to and feels familiar. You may not even know once you're in a relationship in adulthood that your significant other is doing this because it's your comfort zone. This is also why people stay in physical or verbally abusive relationships. If their childhood involved this kind of abuse, it's feels familiar even though you know it's wrong. We always tend to go towards our comfort zone.

Here are some signs of controlling behavior in a relationship:

1) They are always calling or texting you excessively and then get upset if you don't respond right away.

2) They want to know where you are and you who are with all the time.

3) They ask you to make a date with them during a time frame that you told them previously you had plans with others. Then they try to get you to break your plans or try to join you instead.

4) They try to make you do things you are not comfortable with or stated you don't want to do.

5) They get upset when you don't comply with their demands and explode with rage or try to make you feel guilty.

6) Despite your opinions they are always right and you are always wrong.

7) They won't listen to your opinions or ideas.

8) They cannot have a conversation and see both sides of the coin; it's their way or the highway.

9) After one date they say you are in an exclusive relationship with

them without having a discussion about it. If you go on dates with other people after the fact they freak out.

It may feel flattering in the beginning that someone is giving you all this attention, but it's not healthy attention. It's actually very unhealthy behaviors. Within the first week of dating someone, no one needs to know your daily itinerary minute by minute. That's creepy for one. Second of all, no one is in an exclusive relationship until the two people sit down and have a discussion about it. That's something the two of you decide together, not one person telling the other person you're only dating them.

Example of controlling behavior: My father wanted me to do a nasal rinse when I was having sinus problems one day. I didn't want to just for the pure fact that I didn't want to squirt something up my nose. He slammed the nasal rinse and plastic syringe on the countertop and yelled at me to do it. I said no; he screamed back, "I must not know anything then!" and marched off pouting like a child. It was kind of funny; what's the big deal? I just didn't want to do it. Later that night we went to a friend's going away party. Two of my friends at the party were both doctors. My father went up to them and said I needed to do a nasal rinse to help my sinuses and asked their opinion. Then he tried to get her to convince me to do the rinse. She came over to me and told me what their conversation was about. I rolled my eyes and told her I just didn't want to and didn't understand why he was so bent out of shape about it. We laughed, and yes maybe it would help my sinuses, but the point was I just didn't want to. My father responded like it was the end of the world if I didn't do what he told me to.

Controlling behavior feels like you're a caterpillar in a cocoon struggling to get out and spread your wings, yet the other person wants to keep you in your cocoon. The more you struggle to get out, the tighter they hold you in. If you do break out for a while they will try even harder to hold you down until you finally get weak and just give up.

If you feel like you're constantly struggling in your relationship and they are showing any signs of controlling behaviors from above, get out. You are the only one who will allow someone to control and manipulate you. Stop letting someone else control your life.

Most people who feel the need to control others will not want to have anything to do with you unless they can control you. It's better to walk away and end the relationship if you can for your sanity. If the person is a family member or co-worker, try to keep them at arm's length. When you must interact with them, try to keep the peace. Though, as soon as they start bossing you around just end the conversation and walk away. They will soon realize you will not tolerate this kind of behavior.

How to eliminate others controlling you:
1) Don't answer their text messages or phone calls.
2) If you must speak with them, keep it short and end the conversation if they start telling you what to do.
3) Don't tell them your daily itinerary if they ask, just say I'm working or I'm going out. Don't say with whom or where you are going.
4) If they keep trying to contact you obsessively or get nasty, turn your phone off if you need to.
5) Don't respond to their emails.
6) If you met them on an online dating site, block them so they cannot see every time you log on.
7) If you added them on Facebook, delete them. With social media it makes it very easy to stalk someone.
8) Don't allow them to make you feel guilty

Just remember that you cannot change someone else, you can only change the way you allow others to treat you.

Manipulating Behavior

In manipulating behavior, one person tries to muddle the thoughts of the other person. They get inside your head to make you think that your opinions, ideas or thoughts are not logical. You must be crazy, why would you think of such crazy accusations? They don't want you to be able to trust your own instincts. You are always confused and your thoughts murky because they are trying to control you with your own mind. They will slowly pick away at you and try to break you down so you believe everything that they say.

For instance, my second fiancé cheated on me during our engagement period. Despite this I still trusted pretty much everybody, maybe even a little too much. Most people start having trust issues once they have been cheated on, but for me I did not. I somehow managed to escape unharmed in that area. Once I started dating my soon to be husband a year or so after that, I had some feelings that he was being unfaithful. I didn't really have any hard evidence; it was just a gut feeling inside of me. We were engaged, but not living together. We spent a lot of time together, but he also had his son from his previous marriage whom lived in Miami. Being the good father I thought he was, he would travel to Miami frequently to see his son. Sometimes I would go with him and sometimes I would stay back in Tampa to have weekends with my girlfriends.

Back then MySpace was more prevalent than Facebook (I had actually never even heard of Facebook at the time), he and I both had separate MySpace accounts and utilized it frequently with other friends and family members. My cousin deleted her MySpace account and created a Facebook one after breaking up with a longtime boyfriend. Once she told me this I started searching on Facebook for her and surfing the site to see what it was about. One day I searched my fiancé's name and his profile popped up. It wasn't even private; it was all out there for everyone to see. My heart dropped into my stomach as I browsed his information. He listed his first name as his middle name instead. The location stated that he lived in Miami and not in Tampa where he really resided. His profile was littered with photos of just himself flexing and posing for the camera. His status said single and all his friends were females. I was completely enraged!

I immediately called him and demanded to know what the hell was going on. He laughed and said I had nothing to worry about. That made me even more furious, why would he have a profile for no reason filled with lies? That made him defensive and turned the tables back on me. He said I never trust anyone since my fiancé before him cheated, that I was delusional and freaking out for no reason.

I'm sorry but no man would have a Facebook profile with false names, false locations and only picture of him flexing unless he's trying to hook up with other women. Of course he can't state that he's engaged on there; that would ruin his game! I had probable cause to not trust him when he's putting stuff like this out on the internet, portraying himself as a single guy living in Miami.

Even though my gut said this is all wrong, what is going on here, he kept telling me that I was the crazy one. There was something wrong with me. That I had no reason to feel the way I did. He kept making me not trust myself. That's when you know someone is trying to manipulate you. They turn the situation around on you and block you from your own intuition. That's one of the strongest attributes someone has within themselves. Never let someone tell you what you feel is wrong. Always trust your gut instincts; they are there for a very good reason. Of course eventually down the line, I did find out he was cheating on me pretty much throughout our entire relationship. My feelings were dead on.

Another sign of manipulating behaviors is when the other person keeps turning the tables so they always win or come out on top. No matter what you say or do, they change the situation so you are wrong and they are right. That you are the one that made them do the bad behaviors, you are the one to blame not them. You didn't have enough sex with them so that's why they cheated. Or you made them feel uncomfortable and that's why they wanted to move out. They will not accept any responsibility for their own behaviors.

For example, I had only gone on one previous date with a guy from Morocco. A few days later he wanted to take me out to dinner, yet I already had two parties that I was attending that night which he was aware of. During the second party he wanted to know if I want to meet him up later at a night club. I told him my girlfriends and I was going to a club in downtown St. Petersburg. He wanted us to go to Tampa and I said no, were not changing our plans at the last minute. We had already discussed amongst my friends and I what we were doing that night.. He wanted to join us and I said that was fine.

My friends and I were at the club for about an hour or so when he showed up with his brother. Most of my other friends left to go home at that time, I and one other girlfriend stayed there with him and his brother. After only one drink together my girlfriend got upset and wanted to leave. I wasn't really sure what the problem was, but I wasn't going to leave a girlfriend by herself late at night. So I said okay, let's get a cab back. She was very distraught and said she wanted to go home by herself. So I asked the Moroccan guy if he could take me to my house. I made sure my friend got into a cab okay and then he drove me over to my place. I felt kind of bad because he had driven a long way out there, yet I was upset because my girlfriend was upset and I wasn't really sure why.

When he got to my house, I invited him in for a drink, yet he said he had a long drive ahead of him and declined. Then he stated I should get some rest because it was late. I agreed and he left. The next day he was upset at me for not hanging out with him longer the night before. I told him I didn't know my girlfriend was going to get upset and sometimes life happens and it's out of your control. It wasn't my fault, but I did invite him over afterwards and he didn't want to.. He wasn't very understanding and instead tried to make me feel guilty. Then continued on about how we were supposed to hang out that weekend. I told him: I had plans, and sometimes things don't always go as planned. No matter what I said, he kept turning the tables on me. There was no way he was going to understand. The weekend didn't go the way he wanted it to so he was going to blame me anyway he could spin it. However no matter what he said, I would not allow him to make me feel guilty. I had done nothing wrong so I was not going to apologize.

Don't allow someone to spin the tables on you. Listen to what makes sense. Life happens, things change, everyone needs to be able to adapt. Yes, sometimes we drive long distances for nothing. I have been in real estate for 10 years. I can't even tell you have many times I have driven an hour to a property to show it and the clients never showed up, no calls, and no cancelations. It is irritating, but what can we do? That's life; things don't always go as planned.

Are You Over Functioning?

Everywhere I go, I see women over functioning. I can spot it well because I, too, used to over function. It's very easy to do. You like a man; you want to do everything for him. From the beginning of your first date, you want to plan where you're going. You're even willing to drive over to his part of town to meet him, arranging all the details so everything is perfect........for him.

Unfortunately, all this does is turn him off and push him away. It makes it way too easy for him, and you never allow him to do anything for you. When he becomes distant, stops calling and texting, you freak out and put over functioning into overdrive. Your mind goes crazy, *why isn't he calling? Why isn't he texting? I've done everything right, been perfect, planned our dates flawlessly, I sent him sweet messages every day; what's wrong?*

What's wrong is now you've turned into a hair short of a crazy stalker. You have pretty much pushed him away and over the edge, completely squashing any desire he had left inside himself for you. What you need to do is RELAX. Stop everything you're doing for him and start concentrating back on you. Stop calling, stop texting, stop sending Facebook messages, stop everything. Get back into your routine of working out, hanging with your girlfriends, working, going to the beach or getting manicures.

Stop obsessing about him and start taking care of yourself and he'll magically all of a sudden start taking interest in you. He'll start planning dates for you, asking how your day was and sending you sweet messages. If he doesn't, then he wasn't worth your time anyway. He was just hanging out with you because it was convenient for him.

I went to a baseball game with a fella, and we were sitting next to another couple. At first, I had no idea if they were married or just dating. During the game, we chatted a little bit and I noticed the man wasn't wearing a ring. As I watched the game, I also monitored the couple's interaction. When the guy walked to the concession stand, I struck conversation with the woman. I learned she was living in Boston, and he lives here in Florida. She came down to visit him and see the Red Sox and Rays play.

They are in the early stages of dating, but I'm not sure how long they have been together. My interest was piqued more because this is obviously a new relationship for them. I had noticed previously that she was always getting up, going to the concession stand and bringing them back beers. First time, no big deal. Second time, she's nice. Third time, wow she really likes this guy. Fourth time, OK honey, you're dramatically over functioning! Not to mention the beers at the Tropicana Stadium are $8 a piece, and every time she was getting up she was dropping about $20 if you include a tip.

The girl was about my age (early 30s) with a pretty face, a nice figure and a sweet disposition. You think this guy appreciated the fact that she threw down $100 for him and basically waited on him hand and foot, bringing beers the entire game? Nope, not at all. He was actually rude towards her. The last time she served him beer, he uttered in a condescending tone, "Really more beer?" I turned to my date and told him, "That couple over there, it's never going to work out!"

Over functioning does not discriminate age, race or creed. On the Fourth of July, I witnessed another woman over functioning on a first date. My friends and I were sitting at a beach bar having some drinks, listening to a live band and waiting for the fireworks. As nightfall grew closer, the bar became more packed and sitting room was at a premium. A couple in their early 50s walked by us and found a table with only one chair. The man just stood there drinking his beer doing nothing. The woman went off in search for an additional chair for him to sit. We had a few extra chairs so she came over to our table and asked for one. I said sure, and she responded that this was the first date she had been on in 10 years and she wants everything to go perfect. She carried the chair back over to the table herself, the man sat down in it and then waited for her to buy more drinks. Once the fireworks started and everyone at my table was cuddled up with their dates, oohing and awing, this over functioning woman was sitting at their table alone.

Once you stop over functioning, you allow the man room to breathe. When you do too much for him, you are smothering him. You are doing the chasing and most men do not like to be chased. The ones that do are lazy and that's not the kind of guy you want to have a long-term relationship with. Men need the chase. They want the one woman that no man can tame or catch. If you make it easy on him, then he loses interest. If you're a valuable prize that he needs to compete for, he will treat you like gold and take care of you because he knows if he did no less, someone better out there would claim his prize.

Listen to Your Dreams

If you're not sure where your relationship is going, dreams can tell you a lot about what's going on in your life. When the body rests the subconscious mind will allow thoughts to emerge at night that during the daytime your consciousness will not allow. Relax, stop over thinking and let your mind do the work.

For example, while I was married, the entire last year or so I kept having bad dreams about my husband. I was in a panic state of mind during my dreams that I couldn't find him. The dream would always start off as us entering into a very crowded theme park, and then I would see the back of his head as he disappeared into the crowd. I would call, text, yell out his name but he would never respond and I could never find him. Waking up in a panic, I would look over and he was there lying in bed right next me. Then one day my dream became a reality when he was off in Miami staying with a woman he was cheating on me with. The same sickening feeling arose in my gut from the dream when I kept calling him with no answer, but this time for real. As soon as the truth was revealed, the dreams stopped.

After my divorce I went on vacation to Vegas with a few girlfriends. The first night we were there a man approached us in a bar. He was good looking air force guy from Great Brittan. His game was pretty intense from the start, wooing me, getting my phone number, trying to date me from the first night. We hung out during the weekend, then he said he was going to be stationed in Miami for a month and wanted to visit me. I thought *why not*? After we both left Vegas, I never heard from him again and started having those weird dreams again. I figured he was probably married and just looking for some excitement when he's out of the country. Good thing nothing ever transpired between us.

In another situation I was dating a man I thought I had a great connection with. Though, the last few dates we just weren't clicking. The last date wasn't fun. My irritation levels were at an all-time high and I just frankly felt bad about the whole situation. I had been tossing the idea around for a bit that we should see other people. Then that night I had a dream that I kept losing my shoes. I was in various situations where I would have one shoe and kept searching for the match to my pair. Sometimes I was in a department store or other times in someone's backyard. When I woke up it hit me, he's not my soul-mate. I still need to keep looking for my perfect fit.

The most important thing to take from this chapter in weeding out the right one for you is to see how you feel after spending time with someone. Do they make you happy and feel good about yourself? Do you want to go run to the mountain tops and scream to everyone how happy you are? Or does the person make you feel bad about yourself? Start listening to your feelings / instincts and stop over analyzing every little thing that happened on the date. We need to get more in tune with our own feelings and emotions. The answer is usually buried within there.

The Power of Words

One of the reasons I love writing is because of the subtle power of words. Simple letters placed on a piece of paper or spoken can have such a great impact. Words can start wars or they can create peace. They can build someone up or tear them down. It can make someone fall in love or break their heart. Words can make you believe in yourself or slice through your flesh like mini razor blades.

We all need to be very conscious of what we say and who we say it to. You may not even realize the words that come out of your mouth will have a great impact on the person who hears it, but it does. It doesn't matter how young or old you are, words still hurt. Usually the older we get the more we understand that what another person says is more or less a reflection of them. That they may say something ill-hearted because they are just un-happy with themselves.

When you start dating someone pay attention to how you speak to them and how they speak to you. Verbal abuse is very prominent in our society and I see it everywhere. Unfortunately, it's not as easy to detect as physical abuse, yet I think it hurts worse. I do because they are little slices on the inside of us that slowly chip away at our self-esteem.

Sometimes you don't even realize the damage until it's too late and going to your doctor to get some Zoloft. However, verbal abuse is much easier to stop versus physical. You just have to be the one to put your foot down and walk away.

For instance, say you start dating someone and you're still trying to get a feel for their personality and them for yours. You joke around and make silly comments, no harm no foul. Then they say something that catches you off guard, "Gee that bleach from your blonde hair must have soaked into you skull and killed some brain cells!" Ouch! That hurt, not your scalp that is. It hurt on the inside. It wasn't very funny and you find it offensive. The first thing you have to do is immediately hold them accountable for what they said so they don't forget. Confront them head on, politely respond, "That wasn't very funny and it hurt my feelings."

Now, to find out if this person is actually verbally abusive *or* is just pushing the jokes to the edge; pay attention to how they respond when you call them out on it. If the person responds with, "I'm so sorry, I didn't realize I was being mean. I thought we were just joking around." If they answer this way and you can tell it's sincere by their tone and gestures, then all is well. No one is perfect and some people's humor is a bit off. What's important is that they *care* about you and your *feelings*. These are your feelings, no one can tell you what to feel. Also make sure they don't make similar jokes again.

Instead if you confront them and it goes more like this, "What is wrong with you? Don't you know I'm kidding? Why are you being such a cry baby! You are so sensitive, get over it!" Then they do not have your best interest at hand. That person does not care about your feelings and if they hurt them. They will try to make you feel guilty about the emotions you have. This person is verbally abusive. It doesn't matter how many times you confront them or tell them what they say hurts you. It will always constantly be an emotionally draining battle with them and what's lost in the end is your self-worth. It's easier to end the relationship and find a healthier person. If you're verbal abuser is a family member or co-worker try to keep them at an arm's length. Only communicate when necessary. If they start becoming verbally abusive, stop the conversation by hanging up the phone or walking away.

Words can be deadly weapons. Please use them wisely when speaking with anyone. Use words for good to help, inspire and uplift people. Like they say, if you don't have anything nice to say, then don't say anything at all.

From the Y Chromosome

1) Are you still single or are you in a relationship currently?

Dan – 56 – in a LTR: *"I've been in a committed relationship for one and a half years now. We live together without any kids. She was married for four years previously."*

Nathan – 28 – Single: *"I'm currently single. I'm just looking for someone to hang with right now. It would take a while for me to decide if I want to be in a committed long term relationship with someone."*

Chris – 41 – Divorced: *"My divorce is just getting to the finalization stages. I've gone on dates from online, though I don't really think I'll meet my future wife on one. Maybe I will through someone I've met online, such as one of their friends. I'm just taking this experience as I'll be able to meet new people and make new friends, expand my social circle."*

Jerry – 60 – in a LTR: *"I am in a relationship with a lovely lady for 18 months now."*

2) Where did you meet the person you're with now? What sets them apart?

Dan – 56 – in a LTR: *"We met on Match.com. Our first date was on her birthday. She's 37 years old but looks much younger. She gets carded all the time. I like her because she's sweet and innocent, never raises her voice. We have never had a fight in our entire relationship. She loves animals and gets emotional when an animal is being harmed because it's not their fault."*

Jerry – 60 – in a LTR: *"I met her on Match.com. I had been on the site* *since the beginning of it. I have probably written to over 1,000 women and meet face to face at least 100. Several turned into wonderful friendships, some relationships and some just didn't work out. The lady I'm with now had basically given up on dating. Her daughter who was 26 at the time said she needed to get out there and meet someone. So her daughter posted the profile. She got 100 responses in one day. Her daughter weeded out the men and narrowed it to three and then my lady chose me. We meet at the chick-a-boom room and had a great time. She looked just like her profile. Usually I dated women 5-10 years younger than myself. She's closer to my age, and doesn't have the blue eyes I adore, yet it didn't matter because we just clicked. I knew I was going to give it a chance and now we're exclusive. She has a great sense of humor and gets my warped funny side. She loves the fact that I'm Jewish even though she's not. Her top personality trait is that she's so sweet, she's my angel. It took me 18 years to find her."*

OVERVIEW: Rule #7

- If it's not clicking by the third date, move on to save everyone time.
- Don't get stuck in the "nice guy" stereo type, judge people on their actions rather than words.
- Utilize dating tests to see if this is the one for you.
- If you see signs of controlling or manipulating behavior early on, get out!
- Stop over functioning.
- Listen to your feelings.

RULE #8
GOING BACK ON DATING SITES

Your first date with MR. GQ#9 was fantastic. He was good looking, witty, fun, and your knees go weak when you looked into his eyes. He asks you out again after your coffee date. You blush and accept. Two dates turn into three and four, now it's an adult slumber party. Everything seems great, then all of a sudden a month into it, you notice how he scrapes his fork against the plate while eating. He sounds like a bear in hibernation during the night and your work is taking a back seat to your afternoon naps to catch up on sleep. The two of you are arguing about simple things like where to go for dinner. Finally you just snap and can't do it anymore. It simply doesn't click like it did in the beginning. It's time for the talk.

Within the internet dating jungle, sometimes you find someone worth hiding your profile for a while to see where the relationship develops. It may last a week, a month or a year. Then you discover that this person just isn't the one for you. It's time to put your profile back up and start from square one. There's no point in trying to force the issue if it just isn't there. It's not fair to both persons involved in the relationship. Everyone deserves to have someone who can give their all.

If you realize soon into dating someone that their little quirks just get under your skin, it's probably not going to work out long term. It's best to just be honest and move on. There is someone out there for everyone and that just wasn't the person for you. Don't beat yourself up if it doesn't work. Everything needs to click just like a key into a lock. If one pin is out of place, the key will not open the door. You can try to pick the lock to force it open, but that's just a lot of effort. The key should slide perfectly into the lock, clicking all the pins into place to smoothly open the door.

When you go back onto dating sites it's important that you update your profile. Even if it has only been a couple of months, things have changed. Hopefully you have learned from the last relationship so you can better understand what it is you are looking for. Nothing is ever lost from an experience.

You should always update your photos while changing your written profile. Granted you have probably not gained or lost a ton of weight or drastically altered your hairdo, but fresh pictures are important for a few reasons. For one, having them up-to-date as possible means you are truly representing yourself. You may think you look the same as you did last summer, but others may beg to differ. Also, when reactivating your profile, if you post new photos you will attract new people to your page. If you always have the same photos people will just pass you by if they have read your profile once before. Rotate your photos and you will generate new interests. Remember to always have at least one close up facial photo and one full length body pose. Wear appropriate clothing, too, please. If you post a boob shot, or a slutty dress, don't be shocked by emails from guys only interested in one night stands.

There will probably be many of the same people on the same sites again. To me, internet dating seems to be similar to dating in a small town. I met my ex-husband on a dating site. I had dated various men from other dating sites prior to marrying him. I was off the internet dating market for four years. When I embarked upon them again, the same men were still on the same sites with the same photos. It felt like those four years never happened. It was very surreal. I could remember who I had chatted with and who I had gone on dates with. They would send me messages like they had no idea who I was. If it didn't work out four years ago, there was really no point in trying again.

I'm not sure if any of these men remembered messaging me or not. However, I felt it was rude and more embarrassing for them if they didn't. Now, I know you cannot remember every person you email, yet if you have a long drawn out conversation with someone and meet them in person, you should be able to recall who they were. I recognize the same people from website to website. There are a few ways you can remember who it was you have already chatted with. I might as well save you some time with notes and research. I keep mental notes, though I never forget a face, so if we chatted at any length of time I will remember you.

Funny Dating Story

I met a man from POF while my mom and brother were down visiting Florida for a few months, in February, to get away from the cold Nebraska winter. This man and I had extended conversations online before he asked for my cell phone number. Once I gave it out, we texted constantly. He said he was divorced with no kids and was a high school teacher who had a twin brother. They used to wrestle professionally together prior to both becoming teachers. Being typical identical twins, they even purchased houses right next door to one another and became married around the same time.

I lived about an hour north of me and it was hard to schedule any dates. For some reason he could only come late at night and didn't stay for very long. For our first date we were supposed to meet for dinner. He was three hours late and I started drinking some wine at home. I completely blew him off and figured he was standing me up. He said his best friend called him and said she was going to commit suicide, so he had to pull his car over on the side of the road and talk her out of it. I pretty much think that was a line of bullshit. Though, he was very persistent in still wanting to hang out, so I was like whatever. I met him out for about 30 minutes and was totally annoyed the entire time. He left but continued texting me.

I decided to implement my "three strikes, you're out policy" and give him the benefit of the doubt. So we continued to chat and arranged to meet in the coming two weeks by the beach. Once again, he was late. I even left the beach condo my mom was staying at 30 minutes after we planned for dinner just because I assumed he would be late. Even then I still waited about 45 minutes for him to show up. I was almost ready to walk out the door when he appeared. He apologized and said he was sorry and gave me some lame ass excuse I don't remember. We ate dinner then he excused himself to the bathroom. He occupied it for way too long unless he was shaving his entire body.. When he finally emerged he was acting fidgety and nervous. I know I can make some men uneasy (being on a date with a dating coach and all), yet there was something else going on. He walked me to my car and gave me the smallest peck in the history of kisses.

Putting all the pieces of the puzzle together, I suspected that he was probably still married and not divorced like he told me. Why else was it so hard for him to make and keep plans? Why was he always so late? Why was he in the bathroom for 20 some minutes? I didn't even do the research to find out if he was; I just trusted my gut instincts on this one. Something smelled like a rat and I wasn't going to stick around to find out what it was.

Almost a year later I have been flopping back and forth between OkCupid and POF, doing research, going on dates and so forth. Funny enough I just received an email the other day from an account with no photo. I never email guys without a photo because they obviously have something to hide. Though, for research purposes I replied to this one. He stated in his email that he was in education and he couldn't put his photo out there because his students might be on the site. So I asked him what he did and he said he's a high school teacher and used to be a professional wrestler with his brother.

Save yourself the embarrassment of the wrestler, that's the worst move in the dating world, to not remember someone you went out with previously. Give people the credit that they do remember you. A better way to contact someone that you previously chatted with before, maybe even a year or so prior is to send an email like:

"Hi how are you? You're looking well these days. We chatted awhile back and I was just seeing how you are doing? We never had a chance to actually meet in person and I would like to see if we could now?"

Or

"Hey how have you been? I see you're back on this site, as I am too. I had a nice time when we went out a while ago and I was wondering if you would like to meet up again?"

Acknowledging that you remember the person is a much better route than pretending like you have no idea who they are. It actually offends me when a man I've had encounters with emails me like I'm a stranger. I don't respond to them. Gee, I guess I wasn't really that special. I didn't stand out from the crowd? Just another case of love spam.

On the same note, when you are chatting with a few different people online make sure to keep yourself organized. It's easier when you are conversing within the dating site because you see their photo. Once you exchange phone numbers and start texting it can get confusing once you start circular dating (I'll define this later). Everyone is chatting with a few guys or girls, setting meet-n-greets, and talking on the phone. Make sure not to confuse Sara with Tara or Jamie with Jeremy.

If you have a smart phone it makes keeping your contacts organized very simple. What I like to do is take a screen shot of their profile picture from the dating site app. This of course only works with POF, OkCupid or if your site has a mobile app. I then save that photo to their contact information. I, of course, put their name in and then in the notes field I enter either their username, what website I met them from, age, occupation, and any other notes I want to keep on them. It definitely helps out so that if you get a random text message from a Chris, and you have 10 contacts with the same name, you open their information and you'll know exactly which Chris it is. During the phases of circular dating, and prior to being in a committed relationship, it's a great tool.

Some people may say this is a serial dater, or a player, but it's not. You have to date until you find the one to spend the rest of your life with. There is nothing wrong with going on multiple dates. That's what you have to do to narrow down the field and find someone you have chemistry with. It would be great if I could chat with one great guy online, meet him for coffee, sparks fly and I know he's the one. Unfortunately that's not reality. How many frogs must you kiss before you find the one? I have kissed way too many! I wish I didn't have to, believe me, yet this is how the cookie crumbles.

Circular Dating

Rori Raye coined this term within her eBook and a website with dating advice. She has some good concepts that I really like, one of which she calls "circular dating." (You can find more information on her website: www.havetherelationshipyouwant.com.) The basic concept of circular dating is that no man or woman should date only one person at a time. Also, don't get attached to just one person from the first date on. This is a completely different concept of sleeping with multiple people. That obviously isn't a good idea. I'm not talking about being a whore; I'm talking about going on lots of short meet-n-greats and then longer dinner dates until you find the one worth spending your time with. Until you have the talk of exclusivity, everyone is open to do what they want.

The problem with most women is that we get attached after just one short date. In our head we are already committed. We place everything else on hold in our lives to see where it's going to go with this man. We start investing tons of time and energy into this relationship and lose ourselves in the process even though there has been no talk of serious commitment. We do this even when we have no idea what the man is really thinking and we just assume he is on the same page as us. We invest our hearts and many times our body. Women look at sex as a cementing of the relationship and then find out a few months down the road he's been dating other women. We get upset and outraged, but for what? There was never a discussion about exclusivity. Men can't read our minds and we can't read theirs. So whose fault is it?

When you're single and dating, assume that everyone is dating and seeing other people. Don't assume one date is to solidify a commitment. That's a discussion to be had with both parties involved that they want to be exclusive with each other. Until then have fun, go out on dates, and date yourself. Dating yourself is spending time doing the things that you love to do and getting back to you. You need to spend time by yourself and be happy alone before you can be happy with someone else. Dating should be fun, go out and have lots of fun until you find someone to be serious with. If you spend time out with different dates you will discover what it is you *do* want in a partner and what it is you *don't* want.

The great thing about circular dating is that it helps build your self-esteem and it lets you know you have choices. There are tons of people out there in the dating jungle. Just because it doesn't work out with one person, well there's a bunch more out there waiting for you to meet. Don't settle for less. I've been practicing circular dating since after my divorce and not getting hung up on just one person, unless I think they deserve my time. I admit I was like everyone else, love struck after one date. But not anymore; I really analyze and ask myself, "Do I really like him? Do I want to spend time with him? How does he make me feel about myself? Why does he deserve to have my undivided attention?" If a guy doesn't call me back or ask me out again after our date I used to freak out, "Oh no, what's wrong with me? Why did I say that or do this? I should have worn a different outfit!" That was the old me, the new me thinks, "Great he just weeded himself out, saved me the hassle."

Circular dating has also helped me weed through the losers.I know I have options and lots of men interested, I don't wait around for the phone to ring for *him* to ask me out. It sends the message that I am a highly sought after woman and you better bring you're A game or someone else will snatch me up. The ones who can't bring it slowly go to the way side and the ones who have the confidence and drive inside will keep fighting until they get their hunted prize. Men still have the animal instincts; they want a chase, they want a woman that's unattainable to them. If you make yourself easily attainable they get bored. A friend of mine states, "I don't do dates unless I can date someone out of my league."

Now don't fear if you're not the most attractive person out there in the dating jungle. There is someone out there for everyone. I'm a strong believer in that. You just need to find the right person for you. Obviously the better looking people get more options, yet having a high self-esteem and sense of self-worth goes a lot longer than just being beautiful on the outside. Really anyone who's disciplined can eat healthy, go to the gym, get a nice body, buy great clothes and get their hair done. I personally think that's the easy part. I figured that out in high school. I was a nerdy kid, tall and overweight. I grew up in a single parent household and we ate lots of fast food. I didn't work out, dressed like a Tom Boy and played the cello. I had my group of friends, yet boys didn't notice me. Once I got my driver's license I starting going to the gym, working out, counting my calories, bringing my own lunch to school, and lost 40 pounds. I wasn't much into fashion, yet I did my research and from reading magazines, watching TV and other kids I basically faked it 'til I made it. I completely transformed myself from nerdy, tall overweight Tom Boy to being voted Most Desirable Female of the Senior Class.

Now all of a sudden I was good looking, all the boys noticed me in school, and everyone asked me out. I had new popular friends and an entire new life. No more nerdy, cello player. Welcome hot-n-sexy diva! Yet, I had only worked on my outside. My inside was still the same, insecure, low esteem Tara. I had a boost of esteem for a while, but it seriously took me until the age of 34 years old to make over the inside. People can tell when you're insecure, shy and nervous. It doesn't matter how good looking you are on the outside, your insecurities will show through. So take some time to work on you. Make you feel good. A happy person looks 10 times better than a good looking sad person.

You Complete Me.... No, I Complete Myself

Long gone is the age old saying, "You complete me." You shouldn't wait around for someone to complete yourself. In a healthy relationship it takes two whole human beings coming together. I was watching The View while waiting in the green room for my live ABC interview the one day and the ladies were talking about women's self-esteem. They quoted Kim Kardashian as stating that she gets her self-esteem from her now boyfriend Kayne West. Whoopi Goldberg then appropriately asks, "If the self-esteem comes from him, when they break-up does he take it with him?"

It's a great statement and reason why you should never place your self-worth in the hands of someone else. Yes, your boyfriend, husband and or wife may make you feel good about yourself, but if you're in a toxic relationship they can also make you feel like crap. That's how controlling people cut you down so you don't think you deserved to be loved and makes it hard to leave abusive relationships.

Now let's look at it from a different perspective. Let's say you loved yourself 100 percent and made yourself whole. Then men or women could come in and out of your life and you would only be slightly affected. It may be sad if something didn't work out, but that's life. You also would know that you deserve nothing less than someone who treats you like gold and wouldn't allow scum bags around you. All your self-esteem and self-worth came from inside you so then no one would able to take it away from you.

From the Y Chromosome

1) What advice would you give men venturing out into the internet dating jungle?

Nathan – 28 – Single: *"It's not easier that meeting women in person. You think that you won't be rejected or embarrassed; yet in some cases it's harder. Women have their guard up higher versus a coffee shop, since some guys want to be anonymous or lie. You really have to be on your A game."*

Dan – 56 – in a LTR: *"Always pay for the site. Don't wait for women to email you, get out there and start contacting them. You should be on as many different dating sites at once. A minimum of at least three, such as Match.com and POF. Though, a woman shouldn't. If I see the same woman on multiple sites she's probably desperate, hard up for a relationship, or really lonely."*

Chris – 41 – Divorced: *"Be honest, it's going to suck putting yourself out there but still be honest. I hate online dating I don't think it's going to be around long term. I had no idea how bad it was going to be. Women get so bombarded with emails from douche bags, it makes it harder on the rest of us that are nice guys. We need more interactive types of activities where people meet in person."*

Jerry – 60 – in a LTR: *"Just be honest with yourself and what you're looking for. You're going to get rejected, don't take it personally. I was excluded for being 5 feet 11 inches and not 6 feet tall. Sometimes you're just not what someone else is looking for. You have to go out there with a positive attitude. Some really good books to read are; 'Men are from Mars and Women are from Venus.' It explains how the different sexes receive information. It's helped me not only in dating but in business as well. Another good book for women is, 'He's just not that into you.' It* *has really good advice. If a guy wants to be with you he will move heavens and mountains. Women too often make up excuses or men of why they don't return phone calls etc."*

2) How do you keep yourself organized when online dating?

Jerry – 60 – in a LTR: *"I have been utilizing internet dating since before the popular website came out. I remember the very first dating site was AOL Love. You had to be an AOL user in order to be on it. I've used almost every site out there for about 18 years. I created an excel spreadsheet to remember which woman I had contacted, I kept notes on them so if I saw them a year later on a different website I would know if we had chatted or not. No sense in wasting our time if there wasn't anything there. I did email the same women sometimes year or so later. I always stated to the fact that we had chatted in the past. A few women I met up with this way and some I did not.*

OVERVIEW Rule #8

- Don't drag out a relationship if you know it's not the one for you.
- When going back on dating sites, update your photos and bio.
- If you contact persons you've chatted with prior, acknowledge that.
- Practice Circular Dating and don't "assume" commitment from another.
- Make yourself a whole individual, don't wait for someone else to.

RULE #9
STOP MAKING EXCUSES

Getting back out in the dating jungle is scary, especially if you have been off the market for 10-20 some years. Nonetheless, stop making excuses and, like Nike says, just do it! One of my friends who was married for 20 years, and has been divorced now for 10, keeps complaining that she wants a husband. I keep telling her the first step to finding a husband is to go on a date!

She has every excuse in the book: I need to lose 10 pounds, I want to get an eye-lid lift surgery, I need to finish my laser hair removal treatments, I need better photos, and it goes on and on. Granted, she's turning 50 this year, but it's never too late to take control of your dating life. Stop with the excuses! They are just a defense mechanism to put up a wall to not allow someone else in. In order to find love you must first be willing to open yourself up to it. Take your walls down, heal your wounds and start going on dates.

My friend paid for a six month subscription to Match.com and has yet to even go on any dates from it. She keeps saying it's her photos because she thinks she's not photogenic. However I think it's more or less that she's scared and doesn't really know which guys she should go for. You need to date people within somewhat of your realm of possibilities. Granted some people do date out of their league, yet the men that are attracted to her she'll say are old and nasty. Well, I hate to be the one to break it to her, but if you're 50, guys in their 50s and 60s are going to be in your dating pool. Of course there are some guys in their 30s who would date older women, but let's be real here.

I'm 35 and the guys that are in my dating pool are not the same for a woman who's 50. Guys normally like a younger woman, doesn't always work that way, but sometimes does. A general rule of thumb to use is no dating someone who is more than 10 years older or younger than you. So my dating pool is guys 25-45. Her dating pool is 40-60. However I usually don't like to date anyone younger than 30, just because it seems we don't have a lot in common. I have tried a few times to be open minded, yet it never worked out.

Dating websites simply aren't for some people. This is also true for my friend. She may not be the most photogenic person on the planet, but she's still attractive, in shape and has a great personality. Internet profiles don't do her justice because she's a people person. We go out for dinner and drinks and she's talking to everyone in the restaurant. She's getting more phone numbers and contacts than I, 15 years younger because I'm more shy and keep to myself when out.

This is where she feels comfortable and her personality shines through. Though, she doesn't take advantage of it when guys who are perfectly suited for her approach her. I've seen multiple guys, older, nice looking, successful, invite her out and she denies it. This is where her excuses come in. Just like a Jerry Seinfeld episode: he's too tall, he's too old, he's too gray, he just wants to get laid, or his shoes looked funny.

If you're not having good luck on dating websites, maybe meeting people out in person is better suited for you. There are lots of other options out there in the dating jungle. You can attend Pre-Date Speed Date events. You go on multiple, short six minute dates in one setting. Then you get to meet people in person and see if there's any chemistry there, which beats you to the point of endless online emails. It cost around $27 per event depending upon your area. Visit their site to check out events near you at www.pre-dating.com. Use promo code TRPD13 and receive $5 off an event.

Other ways to get out and meet new people is to attend Meet Ups, which has a website dedicated to bringing people together that have the same interests. They have groups for just about anything and singles, too. Some are free and some you have to pay to join. Usually it's no more than $10-15. I've meet a lot of great people from Meet Up and I organize a few groups of my own. I attend a writers group and hold singles events and relationship meetings. Check out their website at www.meetup.com.

If you have more cash to spare than most of us right now in the economy, you can try a Match Maker or Events and Adventures. Match Makers will interview you for a few hours and try to find exactly the kind of person you are looking for. Once they get a good feel, they go through their database and set you up on dates that will be a good fit for you. I went to a service once in my twenties; I don't remember the name of it. It was very expensive though. I couldn't afford to pay the fees, but since I was young and attractive they kept me in their database. I think generally it's an older crowd that uses these services. I did go on one or two dates that I can recall of, none of them were really my type. I know they charge anywhere in the thousand dollar range. Events and Adventures also have a very high fee. I have never personally attended this organization either because how expensive it is. Though I've had a few male friends who called and spoke to a sales person and they were quoted between $1,700 - $2,500. I do not fully know what is all included within these fees. I just hear lots of commercials in the

Tampa Bay Area for them and I know they put on lots of singles events. They do everything from white water rafting to cruises and skiing. It looks like fun if you have the money to attend. Their site is www.lotsofevents.com.

So stop with the excuses! Get your butt off the couch and start meeting people! Give someone, anyone, a chance. You have to start somewhere. My first date after my divorce was a disaster, but that didn't stop me. It's a numbers game, but you have to start with the first date. If it doesn't work out, then onto the next; that's called dating. Keep going on dates until you narrow it down by utilizing my weeding out procedures. Just get out there! This should be a fun process getting to meet new people and do fun stuff.

Funny Dating Story

My nerves were tense as I drove to go on my very first online date after my divorce. He was a little younger than me, very tall and worked at a Jaguar Dealership. His photos were good looking and he seemed to have a bit of an edge to him. He wore a collared shirt with slacks in his profile, revealing just a hint of tattoos underneath. I met him in the parking lot outside the restaurant. As we both stepped out of our cars I first noticed his height as he towered over me and leaned in for a hug. It was a refreshing feeling since my ex-husband was short and he always made me feel self-conscious about wearing heels around him. Heels wouldn't be an issue in this new relationship. We walked towards the entrance and I checked him out from behind and noticed he didn't just have some tattoos, he was covered in tattoos. Shorts displayed the canvas on his legs. This was a bit shocking to me since I have no tattoos or piercings on my body anywhere. I can handle a barbed wire around your bicep or something on your back, but I'm really not a cover-my-body-in-art kind of gal.

We sat down inside and he seemed to be a bit uncomfortable. I guess my choice in restaurants was a tad bit too fancy for his taste. We proceeded to read the menu and make small talk, though I kept starring at his arms that were also covered in ink. It ran all the way from his wrists up to his neck almost touching his ears. The flesh of his ear lobes was being stretched by gauge piercings. Somehow none of this was portrayed within his online profile, not to this extent. I was so curious and busy looking at everything on his body I couldn't even really focus on what was coming out of his mouth. I was fascinated like I was watching a documentary on an indigenous tribe from Africa on the Discovery Channel, wondering how painful those piercings were. The only thing similar I had ever done to that was getting an eyebrow ring when I was 19 during my rebellious time, only to remove it six months after the fact.

I sat there silently observing him, and then he said something that jolted me out of my trance, "So I haven't paid my taxes in about five years. I owed the IRS the whole time I had my roofing business down in the Keys."

I was so shocked at what he was saying because I hadn't really paid attention to anything else prior to that. "What do you mean you didn't pay your taxes?" I asked.

"Oh I was just having too much fun partying and with my business down in Key West a while ago, I decided to keep all the money for myself."

"Well that's really not how it works here in the US. You have to pay your taxes. You can't hide from the government."

"I know that's why I had to move back in with my parents. I owe a huge chunk of money and they are garnishing my wages."

"You live with your parents?"

Wow, now that I actually started paying attention to what was coming out of his mouth I couldn't decide what was worse. The fact that he looked like he just stepped off the pages of National Geographic or that the IRS was chasing him and he still lived with mommy and daddy. I was scared that if this is what's out there for the single male population, maybe I was too quick to file for divorce? Was it too late to turn back? Change the judge's decision?

I sucked it up and made it through the rest of the date, trying to be polite and wanting it to end as soon as possible. We left the restaurant and I went home and laid there in bed thinking what have I got myself into, going back into this crazy dating jungle. Then the tattooed man texted me and thanked me for our date and wanted to follow up with another one. I told him I wasn't interested and he asked, "If I would have touched you, would that have made it better?"

No, that would have made me spray mace at you. I sighed, rolled over in bed, covering my head with my pillow thinking, "This is how the new chapter in my life is beginning"? I better hold on because it's going to be a rough ride.

Be Honest With Yourself

With the deadly glare, Jack Nicholson retorts, "You can't handle the truth!" during the memorable scene from the movie A Few Good Men. This statement is so true because most people cannot handle the truth. Everyone has a perception of themselves and if someone gives them a reflection they don't like, they can't handle it. The truth hurts because we don't want to accept it. If someone is trying to help you or tell you areas that need improving, try to listen.

For example, if you're a guy that feels like every woman you go on a date with disappears and never returns your phone calls or texts, don't get upset if someone tells you why. At least now you know. Maybe you can take that and turn it into something positive and improve yourself. Nothing is ever lost from an experience, yet sometimes our egos get in the way of learning.

If a date doesn't go well, instead of just ignoring the person let them know. Wouldn't it be nice to have feedback from your dates versus dead silence? I'm not talking about ill malice type comments, but truthful. If they ask, tell them. Just be prepared for a possible lashed out response. Don't take it personal. They're just not ready to handle the truth. No one's perfect. I'm not, you're not and neither is George Clooney. He's pretty darn close though.

I know I cuss too much, drink too much and place very high expectations on myself and others. After my divorce I was an emotional wreck and had put on about 20 pounds. It was hard to put myself back out into the dating jungle and going on lots of bad dates. One of which I arrived early and sat at the bar for a drink. I saw him walk by outside and not come in. I texted him and then he came back, he said he had to go move his car. He left and disappeared. I kept texting him thinking he was lost. He finally said I looked nothing like my photos and wasn't interested. I was appalled! I had never been stood up in my life. I was voted "Most Desirable Female of My Senior Class!"

It was a hard pill to swallow. Though, after a while I looked in the mirror and realized I wasn't myself. The emotional turmoil of my divorce had taken a toll on my body. For the year after I was eating my feelings instead of dealing with them and it definitely did not show well. I got determined, started consuming healthy food and exercising again. Six months later I was back to my normal, happy, healthy self. It's not easy to look in the mirror, but every now and then we have to. Take these experiences to learn and grow. We all go through difficult times in our lives, let's make the best of them.

Building Self-Esteem

Self-esteem is such an important part of life in general. It can either make or break you. If you have high self-esteem you can do anything you put your mind to. If you suffer from low-self-esteem, everything is a struggle. You always doubt yourself and your abilities, worrying about what everyone else thinks and getting stuck inside your own head. I know because I used to have low self-esteem and tons of insecurities. Looking at me you would have no idea why I was this way. It seemed I had everything going for me in my twenties: great job, nice car, big house, young, good looking, yet I was miserable on the inside. I was so depressed and hated my life, yet I didn't know why. I was so insecure about how I looked, and worried about what everyone else was thinking about me, I was frozen and couldn't really do anything about it. I know my insecurities came through when dating and I didn't think I deserved to be with a man who was a good person. I didn't think that I deserved to be loved, because I didn't love myself.

I honestly think loving yourself is one of the hardest things to do. That's why having a good solid relationship is difficult because y'all got issues! I have my fair share and no one's perfect. It's more about how we deal with them. Since I've practiced my rules over the last few years and built up my own self-esteem, since mine was torn down from being around negative family members, I can see how many people are so insecure out in the dating jungle. There are so many unconfident and wounded puppies running around. Most of my dates I can clearly see need to do Rule #1 in both my books: healing wounds. I think divorce court should mandate self-esteem building class for everyone who ends their marriage. People who have children must take parenting classes. Why is it we must take a parenting class in order to have custody of children after divorce, yet not in order to get pregnant? Maybe it should be reversed? The same with self-esteem classes should be taking prior to dating or getting married. I'm not a huge religious person, though I do see how marriage counseling that churches require of you preceding to walking down the aisle is not a bad idea.

Building your own self-worth is hard to do and even harder if you didn't grow up in a June Clever, Leave it to Beaver household. Most people I know didn't, as an adult you have to cut the umbilical cord and take responsibility for your own life. Parents are not perfect people either. But do not let them control and manipulate the outcome of who you are. This is your life. Stand up and own it. Only you can determine the outcome. Don't be a victim. Nobody wants to hear you complain, bitch or moan. Negativity gets you nowhere. Life is all about perspective and how you look at things. I could have been the casualty of my divorce and childhood, instead I decided to grow from it and make a business venture and in the process help other people. Make lemonade with the lemons life hands you and every now and then for fun spike it with some vodka.

13 Tips for Building Self-Esteem

The following are tips to help build continuous upward momentum towards higher self-esteem: (written by Jae Song & Tina Su on www.thinksimplenow.com)

1. Start Small - Start with something you can do immediately and easily. When we start with small successes, we build momentum to gain more confidence in our abilities. Each completed task, regardless of how small, is a building block towards a more confident you. What are some small actions you can take immediately to demonstrate that you are capable of achieving goals you've set for yourself? For example, clean your desk, organize your papers, or pay all your bills.

2. Create a Compelling Vision - Use the power of your imagination. Create an image of yourself as the confident and self-assured person you aspire to become. When you are this person, how will you feel? How will others perceive you? What does your body language look like? How will you talk? See these clearly in your mind's eye, with your eyes closed. Feel the feelings, experience being and seeing things from that person's perspective. Practice doing this for 10 minutes every morning. Put on music in the background that either relaxes you, or excites you. When you are done, write a description of this person and all the attributes you've observed.

3. Socialize - Get out of the house or setup a lunch date with a friend. Socializing with others will give us opportunities to connect with other people, and practice our communication and interpersonal skills.

4. Do Something that Scares You - As with all skills, we get better with practice and repetition. The more often we proactively do things that scare us, the less scary these situations will seem, and eventually will be rid of that fear.

5. Do Something You Are Good At - What are you especially good at or enjoy doing? Regularly doing things that you are good at reinforces your belief in your abilities and strengths. I (Tina) can be very efficient with completing errands or administrative work. Whenever I have a few hours filled with ways in which I've maximized my time, I feel highly productive and this boosts the confidence have in my abilities as an organized and efficient person.

6. Set Goals - According to a study done at Virginia Tech, 80% of Americans say they don't have goals. And the people who regularly write down their goals earn nine times as much over their lifetime as people who don't. By setting goals that are clear and actionable, you have a clear target of where you want to be. When you take action towards that goal, you'll build more confidence and self-esteem in your abilities to follow through.

7. Help Others Feel Good About Themselves - Help somebody or teach them something. When you help other people feel better about themselves and like themselves more, it will make you feel good about yourself. See what you can do to make others feel good or trigger them to smile. Maybe giving them a genuine compliment, helping them with something or telling them what you admire about them.

8. Get Clarity on Life Areas - Get clarity on the life area that needs the most attention. Your self-esteem is the average of your self-concept in all the major areas of your life. Write down all the major categories of your life, e.g., health, relationships, finance, etc. Then rate yourself on a scale of 1-10 in each area. Work on the lowest numbered category first, unless they are all even. Each area affects the other areas. The more you build up each area of your life, the higher your overall self-esteem.

9. Create a Plan - Having a goal alone won't do much. Get clarity on your action items. One of the biggest reasons people get lazy is because they don't have a plan to achieve their goals. They don't know what the next step is and start to wander off randomly. When you're baking a cake, it's a lot easier to follow a set of clear instructions, than randomly throwing ingredients together.

10. Get Motivated - Read something inspirational, listen to something empowering, talk to someone who can uplift our spirits, who can motivate us to become a better person, to live more consciously, and to take proactive steps towards creating a better life for ourselves and our families.

11. Get External Compliments - As funny as this point suggests, go find a friend or family member and ask them "What do you like about me?" "What are my strengths?" or "What do you love about me?" We will often value other people's opinions more than our own. We are the best at beating ourselves up for things not done well, and we are the

159

worst at recognizing what we've done well in. Hearing from another person our strengths and positive qualities helps to build a more positive image of ourselves.

12. Affirmations & Introspection - Use affirmations, but in the right way. Some people think that when they're in a slump, using positive affirmations will help them get out of it. I love affirmations, but I've realized you have to use them in the right way. Sitting on your couch and saying "I am highly motivated and productive" does nothing. Say something like "I am sitting here being very unproductive right now, is this the ideal me? What would be my best self?" Your affirmations have to be the TRUTH. Once you're honest, take the first step towards doing the thing, no matter how small.

13. No More Comparisons - Stop comparing yourself to other people. Low self-esteem stems from the feeling of being inferior. For example, if you were the only person in the world, do you think you could have low self-esteem? Self-esteem only comes into the picture when there are other people around us and we perceive that we are inferior. Don't worry about what your neighbor is doing. Accept that it'll serve you more to just go down your own path at your own pace rather than to compare yourself. Pretend you're starting over and begin immediately with the smallest step forward.

Self-esteem comes from self-dominion. The more power you have in getting yourself to take the right actions, the more self-esteem you will have. Your level of self-esteem affects your happiness and everything you do.

What is self-dominion? It is our ability to get ourselves to actually do, what we want ourselves to do; in other words, self-discipline and self-trust. A person who has dominion over themselves has self-integrity – staying true to their words and commitments.

Every time we fail to listen to our inner voice, and do not take action in something that we need to, we lose trust with ourselves and our abilities. This lack of self-faith continues to spiral downwardly as we flounder to fulfill more commitments.

Positive Affirmations

This is a great way to start building up your confidence. I know it sounds cheesy and I think everyone remembers the funny comedic satires *Daily Affirmations with Stuart Smalley* from Saturday Night Live. His famous quote, "I'm good enough. I'm smart enough. And doggone it, people like me." But all joking aside, it really does help. Fake it until you make it. If you keep telling yourself positive messages, eventually you will believe it deep down inside. Kind of like reverse brain washing. In toxic relationships you can definitely be brain washed in a negative way to hate yourself, so why not do the reverse?

When I first started writing my first book, I had so many self-depleting little voices in my head. "You can't do that, no one will ever read your books, just get a real job, you're crazy..." Many of the little voices were my parents, friends, even what I thought other people might be thinking of me. It was tough dealing with those inner demons and to push through. Sometimes I would be paralyzed in a downward self-hate spiral. It's hard putting your life/soul out there for everyone to judge you. I decided to buy a book on creative coaching "Coaching the Artist Within" by Eric Maisel. It is an excellent book and helped me through my ups and downs during the creative process.

He also writes of using affirmations as thought substitutes. Basically stopping a negative thought process and switching it out with a positive. So when you start thinking, "I'm not good enough" replace it with, "I haven't found my purpose yet." I began creating many positive affirmations for myself and being the creative person I am, decided to incorporate them into beautiful pieces of artwork. Instead of having sticking notes on my bathroom wall, I drew whimsical pieces with bright colors and printed them on canvases to decorate all my walls in my condo. Whenever I'm feeling down in the dumps or negativity creeps into my head, I turn to one of my paintings and it fills me with power.

I sell my uplifting pieces of artwork on Imagekind to help others keep a positive outlook on life. You can view and purchase them on: www.tararichter.imagekind.com/Affirmations.

From the Y Chromosome

1) Have you used utilized other services other than internet dating?

Nathan – 28 – Single: *"I have done Pre-Date Speed Date and Lock n' Key events. I think both have their pros and cons. Obviously the pros of online dating are that you can do it from the convenience of your own home and you have thousands of profiles to look through. The cons are either you never hear back from someone you're interested in or you get bombarded by messages from people you aren't interested in. Plus, there are a lot of high expectations when meeting someone from online in person that can be thwarted. With speed dating/lock 'n key, it's great because you are meeting people in person and you have ice breakers, but you can only work with who shows up to the event. Some events can be pricy sometimes, and speed dating can be difficult since you have only a short time to get to know someone."*

Jerry – 60 – in a LTR: *"Yes, I did utilize a Match Maker once. She did a very in-depth few hour long interview to find out what I was looking for. I went out with about three women which were very much my type, she did a good job picking them, yet none of them transpired into any relationship for me. It is fairly expensive service, yet I'm not able to disclose how much I paid."*

OVERVIEW: Rule #9

- Stop making excuses; just get out there!
- It only takes one to spend the rest of your life with, the rest make for funny stories on your journey.
- Be honest with yourself and take constructive criticism to grow and develop.
- Build your self-esteem.
- Create positive affirmations and replace any negative thoughts with them daily.

RULE # 10
FIND YOUR JUNGLE PERSONALITY

In the last chapter of the book are quizzes and activities to help you find out what your dating jungle personality is. Having a better knowledge of who you are will help you find others with whom you mesh. Of course sometimes opposites attract and, other times, being similar is boring. You want to find a good fit for you. In the animal kingdom there is a hierarchy of social status. Some are the natural born leaders, then second in command, and so forth. It brings a natural order in a community. There are six ranks given special attention in ethology and been given applicable names:

1. Alpha
2. Beta
3. Gamma
4. Delta
5. Epsilon
6. Omega

Wikipedia states the Alpha animals are given preference to be the first to eat and the first to mate; among some species they are the only animals in the pack allowed to mate. Other animals in the community are usually killed or ousted if they violate this rule. Animals tend to live in groups with a specific social order due to their natural tendency. The leader of the pack is called the alpha male, while there may also be an alpha female depending on the species.

The Betas are the second in command and will take over power if an Alpha dies. The rest are followers of the leaders. An Omega is subordinated to all others in the community. The Omegas might be used as scapegoats.

This hierarchy in the animal kingdom is very similar in our society. Which rank are you? Do you naturally lead others? Or are you more of a follower? Do people tend to listen to you and respect you or do they walk all over you?

Knowing which rank you are in the dating jungle can make it easier for you to find your mate. It would be difficult for an Omega to pair with an Alpha because the strong personality would most likely get too easily bored with the Omega. Figure out what your dating jungle personality is. One isn't better than the other; the key is knowing where you fit. We need leaders and followers in life. Knowing which one you are will just make it easier to survive the dating jungle.

Are you an Alpha, Beta or Omega in the Dating Jungle?

OkCupid.com has thousands of fun tests to take on their site, another reason why I like it. You can look as much into it as you want, or just for fun. They have personality tests to find out which one you are. You can take them online within your profile to add to the content of it and see your compatibilities with others who have also taken them. This test will tell you if you are an Alpha, Beta or Omega. Circle either A, B or C. Then add up the points A=1, B=2, C=3.

1. You and your two friends are hungry and decide to grab a bite to eat. What do you do?
A) I'll do whatever my friends feel like doing.
B) Can't we just get some fast food or something?
C) Let's go to Chili's - the waiters/waitresses there are hot!

2. You mosey outside and get in the car. Who is driving?
A) I'll take the back seat. There's more room and the stereo sounds better.
B) Are you kidding me? Someone else can drive. I call shotgun!
C) Me of course, (and don't touch the stereo)!

3. You pull up to the restaurant, get out of the car, and walk to the door.
A) I take my time. There's no rush.
B) I walk next to my friends.
C) I'm in front of everyone else with my head held high.

4. You've reached the door. What do you do?
A) Hold it open for your friends.
B) Let someone else hold the door for me.
C) Push it open because it's in my way.

5. You're inside waiting to be seated. You...
A) Sit and wait; take in the atmosphere.
B) Cross your arms and stare at people.
C) Get the host's attention. You need a table NOW!

6. You've been seated. What do you do?
A) Put my things (wallet/purse/etc.) on the table.
B) Tell jokes, make small talk, just be.
C) Make fun of that girl's/guy's jacket. What? Who cares who hears me!

7. The waiter is ready to take your order. How do you proceed?
A) I order the same thing as my friend, or just let him/her order for me.
B) I order for everyone else. I already know what they want.
 C) Diet Coke, no ice - and don't forget this time!

8. That waiter/waitress is really cute. What do you do?
A) I didn't expect to meet such a hottie, and my friends look way better. I don't have a chance.
B) Get their phone number.
C) I'm too good for them.

9. The food is here. It's time to eat. You...
A) Ask your friends how their meal is. Maybe they'll let you try theirs.
B) This is boring. Can we go yet?
C) Talk with your mouth full.

10. You've finished your meal. You have some time before the waiter brings you the check. What do you do?
A) Tidy up your area and make pleasant small talk.
B) Stretch out your arms and legs; maybe let loose a big ole' burp!
C) There was ice in my coke! What terrible service!

11. Now for the damage.
A) I'll pay. I insist!
B) I'm willing to pay, but I'd rather split it.
C) They can pay it. They like buying me things.

12. What about the tip?
A) What a nice person. I think I'll leave a little extra.
B) No one has money? Whatever, I'll tip.
C) They already get an hourly wage. What's the minimum gratuity in this state?

13. You're walking back to the car. Someone is getting mugged! What do you do?
A) Get to safety and call for help.
B) Get the robber's attention and tell him to stop... or else!
C) Take him down before he has time to think.

14. This is the last question. It's worth a lot of points, so answer honestly. Are you: tall, charismatic AND successful?
A) I'd like to think I'm at least one of those; otherwise I'm pretty average.
B) No one would mess with me; that's for sure.
C) Yes, all three.

Count up your points. If you receive a total of 0-16 you are an **Omega**. Omega ranks are subordinate to all others in the community, and are expected by others in the group to remain submissive to everyone. They are obedient, polite and loyal. We'd be helpless in society without them. I leave you with an excerpt from Fight Club: "We cook your meals, we haul your trash, we connect your calls, we drive your ambulances. We guard you while you sleep. Do not... @&%$ with us."

If you received 17-30 you are a **Beta**. This rank often acts as second-in-command to the reigning alpha or alphas. They are the enforcer, the "right-hand man," "Johnny on the spot" - but they're not an alpha; not yet at least. They are intelligent, beautiful, and strong and everyone knows it. They've had moments of glory, but most of the time the people that matter don't notice. Hang in there; your day will come!

If you received a 31-42 you are an **Alpha**. Male or female individuals or both can be alphas. Where one male and one female fulfill this role, they are referred to as the alpha pair. Other animals in the same social group may exhibit deference or other symbolic signs of respect particular to their species towards the alpha or alphas. They are both the leader of the pack, people look up to them and respect them. They don't take no for an answer and always get what they want. They can easily dictate others what to do. Some maybe intimidate or scared to confront them. Many envy them and want to be them, some get jealous of their talents easily, but it's only because they want to be them.

Can an Alpha Male and Alpha Female be in a Relationship Together?

Now that you have a better understanding of what personality you are, the question is can similar temperaments be compatible? When two strong personalities come together it can either be blissful or a disaster. The key to a fruitful liaison is a delicate dance of power. It's a rubber band effect of give and take. One partner will be more dominate in certain times, allowing the other to relax. But that person then needs to be able to release control and let it flow to their mate when the time calls for it. If the two alpha lovers can master this, true harmony will result.

On the other hand, if one alpha has issues letting go of their dominant role and never allows the other alpha partner to enjoy control, epic catastrophe can erupt. The lesser alpha will grow restless and give up hope by eventually slithering into a submissive role, which does not feel natural to them and may also turn into depression. Or, they become resentful to their mate for making them be this way and lash out by being verbally or physically abusive. They will struggle and fight to take domination. If every attempt fails, eventually they will grow tired and leave the relationship.

Are You a Love Addict?

Circle yes or no to the following questions. Add up the number of yes replies at the bottom.

1. Are you very needy when it comes to relationships? Y   N
2. Do you fall in love very easily and too quickly? Y   N
3. When you fall in love, are you lost in your head thinking/ fantasizing about them all the time? Y   N
4. When you are lonely and looking for companionship, do you lower your standards and settle for less than you want or deserve? Y   N
5. When you are in a relationship, do you tend to smother your partner? Y   N
6. More than once, have you have gotten involved with someone who is unable to commit—hoping he or she will change? Y   N
7. Once you have bonded with someone, you can't let go. Y   N
8. When you are attracted to someone, do you ignore all the warning

signs that this person is not good for you? Y N

9.Is initial attraction more important to you than anything else when it comes to falling in love and choosing a partner? Falling in love over time does not appeal to you and is not an option. Y N

10.When you are in love, do you trust people who are not trustworthy? Y N

11.When a relationship ends, have you felt your life is over and more than have thought about suicide because of a failed relationship? Y N

12.Do you take on more than your share of responsibility for the survival of a relationship/over functioning? Y N

13.Are love and relationships the only things that interest you? Y N

14.Were you the only one in love in your relationships? Y N

15.Are you are overwhelmed with loneliness when you are not in love or in a relationship? Y N

16.More than once, have you have gotten involved with the wrong person to avoid being lonely? Y N

17.Are you are terrified of never finding someone to love or spend the rest of your life with? Y N

18.Do you feel inadequate if you are not in a relationship? Y N

19.You cannot say no when you are in love or if your partner threatens to leave you. Y N

20.Do you try very hard to be who your partner wants you to be? Will you do anything to please him or her—even abandon yourself (sacrifice what you want, need and value)? Y N

21.When you are in love, do you only see what you want to see? Do you distort reality to quell anxiety and feed your fantasies? Y N

22.Do you have a high tolerance for suffering in relationships? You are willing to suffer neglect, depression, loneliness, dishonesty—even abuse—to avoid the pain of separation anxiety (what you feel when you are not with someone you have bonded with). Y N

23.Do you love romance, having had more than one romantic interest at a time even when it involved dishonesty? Y N

24.Have you have stayed with an abusive person? Y N

25.Do you have fantasies about someone you love, even if he or she is unavailable, and are they more important to you than meeting someone who is available? Y N

26.Are you terrified of being abandoned? Does even the slightest rejection feel like abandonment and it make you feel horrible? Y N

27.Have you chased after people who have rejected you and try desperately to change their minds? Y N

28.When you are in love, are you are overly possessive and jealous? Y N

29.More than once, have you have neglected family or friends because of your relationship? Y N

30.Do you feel an overwhelming need to check up on someone you are in love with? Y N

31.Do you feel powerless when you fall in love—as if you are in some kind of trance or under a spell? Y N

TOTAL:

If you answered yes to 10 or more questions, you are possibly a love addict. So what is a love addict? Wikipedia definition: Like other addictions (drugs, alcohol, gambling, sex, work, etc), the dependency to a person (their object- drug of choice) allows love addicts to feel alive, a sense of purpose and to gain a sense of meaning and self-worth in the world. They are driven by a fantasy hope that the drug of choice - a person - will complete them.

Most love addicts start out attempting to meet some known or unknown emotional need and then become dependent on the intoxicating feelings of being in love itself. Unfortunately, as in the case of drug addicts, "love addicts", too, may become incapable of getting the desired satisfaction, which in turn increases their addiction. They often feel a burning, passionate love that gives and gives, destroying their sense of humanity when they lose the person they've given to, sometimes causing them to feel and act out in a vengeful way. The love addict suffers a lack of bonding as they did in childhood, including an inability to give and receive affection, self-destructive behavior, problems with control, and lack of healthy long term relationships.

Love addicts commonly and repeatedly form an addictive relationship with emotionally unavailable Avoidant partners. The Avoidant partner is compulsively counter-dependent; they fear being engulfed/drowned/smothered by their love addict partner. Love addicts enter relationships with emotionally closed-off individuals who will let nothing and no one in, which makes intimate relationships impossible. Behind their emotional walls, hides low self-esteem and feel if they become truly known (display emotional intimacy) - no one would ever love, accept, and value who they are. Avoidants are attracted to people who have difficulty thinking for themselves, having healthy emotional boundaries, or taking care of themselves in healthy manners- the love addict.

Love addicts and Avoidants form relationships that inevitably lead to unhealthy patterns of dependency, distance, chaos, and often abuse. Nevertheless, however unsatisfying the relationship, love addicts hang on and on, because it is "what they know." Familiarity is the central engine of their relationship. Each is attracted to the other specifically because of the familiar traits that the other exhibits and, although painful, come from childhood.

This cycle encompasses a push-pull dance full of emotional highs and many lows where the one is on the chase (love addict) while the Avoidant is on the run. They both engage in counterfeit emotional involvement. Healthy emotional intimacy is replaced with melodrama and negative intensity—ironically creating the illusion of true love, intimacy, and connection (usually on an unconscious level). As a result, their relationships, although seemingly dramatic in their intensity, are actually extremely shallow.

This quiz and other information have been used from the love addicts website. For more information or help for love addicts, visit their site at www.loveaddicts.org.

Ping-Pong Syndrome

Does your dating life feel more like a ping pong tournament? Are you bouncing back and forth between the nice guy/girl and then back to the bad boy/crazy chick? If so, you may suffer from ping-pong syndrome. If you end up with the crazy chick/bad boy, break it off and find the next safe guy or girl, you may bounce from one extreme to the next.

Stop the tournament and think of the last four relationships you've had. Take a piece of paper and divide it into quarters. Write down each name of the last four people you have dated on each section. Then list all their qualities underneath, good and bad.

Do you see a pattern? Are you bouncing back and forth between two personalities of which neither has worked out in the past? I'm sure each person had good and bad qualities. Now take the good traits from all four relationships and make a new fifth section on the back of the paper. This is the person you should try to seek out, the net in the middle of the ping pong table.

Overview: Rule #10

- Find out what you're dating jungle personality is to become more self-aware.
- Decide if you want to be more dominating, submissive or equal in a relationship.
- Try to find someone that compliments not clashes with your qualities.
- If you're a love addict, recognize certain behaviors so you don't get stuck in the same patterns.

FACEBOOK POLLS

I thought it would be fun to post polls of various dating questions on Facebook to see people's responses. Here are the results! Please take into consideration this is not a scientific study. It's more for fun. I am only using people's first name for the pure fact that you know if it's a male or female responding. Other than that everyone's identity is anonymous.

1) How long should you wait after a break-up to take down photos of your ex on Facebook?
    a. **Nye:** No need to do so if you all had a good relationship. Good memories are always a good thing to keep! Now, if bad memories and guy was a douche, take 'em down now and good riddance!
    b. **Kristie:** My opinion would be immediate take down photos of my ex. To me it's the past and doesn't matter if it's a good relationship or bad. Especially when getting

involved with another person, who wants to see your ex?

   c. **Beth:** I agree with Kristie...I would take them down right away...just so I wouldn't have to be reminded of the past!

   d. **Courtney:** Take them down no need to remind yourself of the past!

   e. **Kyle:** Nothing heals you better than time and space. Why preservative on visual reminders. Keep them locked away on a zip drive where you can access them when you're ready. Nothing hurts a man's pride more than being reminded of your past relationships.

   f. **Nancy:** I left mine for a while. If I liked myself in the picture than it was no problem.

   g. **Kim:** Not that I have that many, but I've not taken down pictures. It's 13 years of my life. I've moved on and I'm not bitter. It wouldn't even cross my mind that it might bother someone I'm dating.

   h. **Colin:** immediately - wash that man right out of your hair.

2) In a new relationship how long do you wait to have sex?

   a. **Kyle:** After drinks

   b. **Chris:** I'm free tonight...

   c. **Lou:** Why wait it will come to an end soon enough once you're married.

   d. **Kristie:** I would wait until the relationship feels like it's going somewhere. I couldn't even stand my current boyfriend now. And look at us 4 years later!! LOL My mother always says, you've got to be friends first before you jump in the sack. LOL It took me a long time to realize she was right!!

   e. **Sabrina:** Wait?? Huh? Lol

    f.   **Pedro:** I'm still holding-out until my honeymoon (i.e. marriage ;-D I'm actually a 37 year-old virgin... **w/ pinky to the mouth like Dr. Evil** Riiight!! Lmao

    g.   **Smitty:** Depends on so many things but never before 2 months of solid dating, but that was years ago, not sure now........

    h.   **Julie:** If you like the way it's going, and are secure enough to take it to the level after the physical part. There will be baggage ..

    i.   **Nye:** As soon as it feels right or you are horny!

3) Do you believe in dating more than 1 person at a time? (not having sex just dating)

    a.   **Nye:** Of course, I am polyamorous. As long as you are open and honest to all you're dating partners.

    b.   **Beth:** If you're not committed then you're NOT committed. But just the dating part...multiple sex partners is very uncool...just my opinion of course.

    c.   **Manny:** SURE WHY NOT.

    d.   **Chris:** As long as you are honest. You can't assume the other person/people feel the same way as you do. So if one thinks exclusive, and the other doesn't and you don't tell each other, bad things are coming.

    e.   **Nancy:** Yes.

    f.   **Colin:** Oh god course, it's a numbers game.

    g.   **Nathan:** Yes.

4) If a date turns into an overnight slumber party and that person had to leave early in the morning for work and trusted you enough to let you sleep in at their place, would you snoop around after they are gone to try to find out what skeletons they have hidden in their closets?

    a.   **Ben:** No. Snooping is creepy. Plus maybe they have hidden cameras and it's a test.

    b.   **Charlyn:** Nah not the first maybe after a week or two.

   c.   **Beth:** NO WAY.... I would most likely leave after waking up at the same time as the person whose home I was at...unless it was a long time committed relationship. I would never put myself in a position to be accused of doing something even. Not my thing...too weird.

   d.   **Emily:** Nah, who cares what they do. Snooping is for married fools.

   e.   **Emily:** lol ^ I meant to say "folks" but that works.

   f.   **Jay:** Snoop all ya want, lol. A good guy shouldn't have anything to hide, and if he's not then @least, you will know soon enough! ahahaha. If you stayed for "an overnight slumber party?" and he's comfortable enough to "slumber 2gthr"?...Then you should make some food while you snoopin. Lol...Rock On! ,J. . _/^"•_•"^_

   g.   **Beth:** No Jay YOU should make some food....it's your place??? Sheesh.. is chivalry dead?? LOL

   h.   **Jay:** No Sweetpea it is not! ....but, her Posted Poll Question stated "He" has left for work.......so, unless he brought her lunch home on his break, "He" wouldn't be able to. So Beth...

   i.   **Jay:** Ya See?......If it were "Me", I would have called in sick, and the "Slumber".....would have Continued!

   j.   **Colin:** Forget responses; I read a study once that said that 40% of people do!

5) If you were on a first dinner date and the other person got something stuck in their teeth, would you tell them? ON THE OPPOSITE SIDE: If you were the one with something in your teeth & discovered it hours later while still on the date, would you be pissed they let you go all night looking like that?

   a.   **Andy:** Yes I'd tell them, it would bother me and I'd expect the same from them. PS, I think you have something in your teeth on your profile pic.

   b.   **Kevin:** Another compelling reason to bring floss to all dinner dates.

   c.   **Kim:** Yes, I would tell them & I'd want them to tell me.

   d.   **Nancy:** Same as above^

   e.   **Smitty:** I'd tell them & want them to tell me! We're human not perfect!

6) How does everyone feel about when guys shave their entire body? Personally I think it's weird men should be men, they have hair; as long as it's not like a sweater what's the big deal? It's also strange when guys rub up on you and you can feel their stubble from shaving.. lol makes me cringe...

   a.   **Ben:** Manscaping is an art form. Unless you're trying to win a swim meet the total hairless look is odd. That said pelvic 70's chic is just gross.

   b.   **Melissa:** stubble is gross.

   c.   **Michael:** How do you define sweater and what's that guy supposed to do?

   d.   **Russell:** I think it started with posers: body builder types, gay models and gothic piercers, then the hairless male look spread through porn, and now...All I know is that if I had to manscape my whole body regularly I wouldn't ever get anything else done.

   e.   **Tara:** Well a sweater would mean when you take your shirt off it looks like it's still on. If you do have a "sweater" then you should at least trim, with buzz cutters. Shorten it up, or cut if it's creeping out the collar.

   f.   **Russell:** Oh I'm not THAT bad. My GF likes the way it is. She hates the hairless look, thinks it's men trying to look like boys.

   g.   **Pedro:** As long as it's not a "permanent thing," (i.e. laser treatments) I'd be Ok w/ it. Many ladies don't care much for back hair thus I get mine waxed every 3-6 months; when I meet a lady that likes back hair, I simply just let it grow back.

h. **Colin:** except for facial hair, never heard a lady ever say anything about men's' body hair, but then I don't have the thick black stuff either...

i. **Pedro:** Chest hair, however, I leave as is ;-p I don't wanna end up in pain like Steve Carell's character from The 40 Year-Old Virgin! Lmao!

j. **Kim:** I'm with you on that! Kinda grosses me out when men shave.

7) How do you feel about sexting prior to meeting an online date in person?

a. **Andy:** Favorable, until you discover she's gross then I feel violated.

b. **Pepper:** Seriously? If you're sexting before you've met, you have problems.

c. **Nancy:** Not a good thing!!!

d. **Angye:** Not Smart.

8) What do you think of a blind/ 1st date on either your b-day or Valentine's Day?

a. **Chris:** High risk, high reward.

b. **Tara:** Interesting, I wouldn't go on a blind date for m b-day (rather be with friends) but might on V day.

c. **Kelly:** No. Too personal to share with someone you don't know or never met.

d. **Chris:** Yeah, but if it works out, you only have to remember one important date and FTD will send out nice reminders. If I could meet, get engaged, get married and have children all on Valentine's that would be great. Not necessarily the same Valentine's day though.

e. **Smitty:** Depends if I had plans but why not..... Who knows what the future will bring!?

f. **Kim:** No way to either. However, I will go to a dating jungle book launch & mixer on Valentine's day ☺

g. **Pedro:** For Valentines' Day I wouldn't mind it as much; because you never know how well we might hit it off & it'd probably be better than spending the day lonely ;'-(I kinda agree with Tara about preferring to hang-out w/ friends on my bday; But what I'd do (depending on what I Do know about her) is invite my blind date to meet up with us.

FINAL THOUGHTS

I believe what you put out into the world comes back to you tenfold. Even if after reading this entire book and you go out on dating websites and write a profile with a negative vibe, that's what is going to come back to you. Or if you write a profile the way you think a guy or girl wants to hear such as, " I just want to go out and have fun" but yet you really are wanting a long term relationship with marriage potential, then you're not being true to yourself. You won't find someone unless you know what you want and be honest in your profile.

Once you start utilizing the rules in this book and my first one, that's when the weirdoes go to the wayside and the winners start showing up. Don't just go out with anyone who asks you out. I used to be that way to give anyone a chance, but that's when you end up with people that are not a right fit you. You have to be picky, you deserve it. Utilize the weeding-out process and use it as a fine tooth comb to narrow down the options with the best potential.

If you treat dating like a lottery system them your chances of finding someone who's a good fit for you is more like getting struck by lightning. Instead narrow it down to only the people with whom you're excited to see in person. Then follow up with the weeding out process during the meet-n-greets, you will greatly increase the probability of finding someone who you are compatible with.

Say you're chatting with someone online more or less because you're just bored. They ask you out and you think why not I don't have plans Friday night and I don't want to sit at home all by myself. The next few days they start irritating the hell out of you and you realize you have nothing in common. If the two of you are both fighting over what to do on your first date, cancel. There's no point. Spatting prior to meeting in person is a red flag, it's not going to get any better in person.

It's similar to married couples who are not getting along so they think having a baby will fix things, no it's just going to make it worse! If you don't have a stable foundation to build on anything you place on top of it will crumble and fall.

Obviously dating and marriage are different yet the same principals apply. If you're not seeing eye to eye in the beginning stages it won't magically get better. You cannot change someone else, you can only change yourself. If you just want to be with that person no matter what, then most likely what will happen is you will end up sacrificing your wants, needs and bending over backwards to make them happy. They won't understand how much of yourself you're giving up to make them happy. You end up resentful and angry and hold them responsible for your unhappiness. In reality if you would of in the very beginning held your boundaries, stood your ground and kept your well-being intact by keeping love for yourself above all you would of seen this person is just not the one for you.

Relationships are like rubber bands you give they may back off a little. You stand your ground they should come towards you. It's a game of give and take. If you stay and they keep moving away and instead of chasing them keep your ground, eventually the rubber band will break. They didn't care enough about you to give a little. Why would you want to be with someone who won't come towards you? It may mean they were only in the relationship out of convenience or loneliness, not from real unconditional love.

One of the most important things I can emphasize that I hope you can take away from this book is that you have to be happy with yourself 100 percent prior to venturing out into the dating jungle. I mean true unconditional love for who you are. No guilt, no shame, nothing. You can wake up in the morning, smile and really be happy at the person looking back at you. Until you can achieve that nothing else is going to matter. It will help you in every aspect of your life. Believe me, I know. I've lived in both ends of the spectrum and until you build up your self-esteem and self-worth, relationships and the world is a very difficult place to live.

Since I've healed myself I see so many damaged, scared and insecure people out in the world. I really feel for them and I want to help them, yet I can't until they decide they want to help themselves. I have lots of people interested in coaching sessions, but yet not sure if they really want to be honest with themselves. It's hard to really open your wounds, it's not fun, being honest with yourself. Though, it's an important step to accomplish to achieve full self-awareness and acceptance.

From the Y Chromosome

After Speaking with a variety of men on the subject of internet dating, my conclusion for the most irritating thing they come across is women who misrepresent themselves. I think this is also true for women. Most complained about issue is that they think they're meeting up with a tall slender hottie with long blonde hair and what shows up is short, chunky chick with choppy brunette hair. I think the bigger issue is not that people *try* to misrepresent themselves, but they really think they *are* that tall hot blonde in their mind. So it's hard for them to understand how they distorted their own image.

This is also another reason why it is so important to get professional, up to date photos to put on your profile. Don't do the ones from high school or college. NOBODY looks the same unless you really are 22 years old. If you keep your pictures within a six month time frame you should look somewhat similar. I mean it's pretty bad when you look at someone's profile and all three photos look like three completely different people. Try not to do the angled backward smart phone pic from high up. I know I'm guilty of this too at times, yet I still include a full body taken from another person and a close facial to include. If you have someone else take the photos it will sow exactly who you are

Even with my photos, guys thought I was petite and skinny.

Those two words have never entered my vocabulary. So I emphasized my height, that I'm muscular and curvy in my written section. I have a chest and an ass, you that's not your type please move on. There are plenty of men who like petite and others who like muscular fit girls. One of the men told me a woman's roommate he dated was a very large lady. She was pretty but had some extra to her. Regular dating sites devastated her. Then she went onto a site for BBW (big beautiful women) and she was in heaven. She had men lined up knocking at her door! Why, because she was honest with herself went to a place where men were looking for what she had. Plain and simple.

My words of wisdom overall to take from this book and out into the internet dating jungle, is just be honest, with yourself and with everyone else. Don't try to be someone you're not. Don't try to do things that you think will make someone else like you. Be you. Love yourself and be happy with you who are. When you stay true to yourself then you will attract someone that loves you for you. That's the best kind of love.

I first started this book during the process of my first one. Then I abandoned it for about six months until I decided to pick it back up again. I always finish a project. Being a quitter has never been in my vocabulary. I'm so glad I did as many people are waiting for its publication.

At the end of my first book I was happy that I approached the tallest, hottest guy in the bar Mr. 6 feet 7 inches. Though, sad to say that nothing did transpire from that encounter. But it did give me courage that I knew I was building up my self-esteem little by little.

I'm happy to say that after utilizing my own rules after about 1 year and 6 months, I have finally discovered Mr. Normal. I think it's the first time ever in my life I have found such a sweet, genuine, caring man in my life. We've know each other now for about 3 months and I keep wondering when he's going to freak out on me or turn into an alien. It's strange after being in so many abnormal, dysfunctional relationships, normal feels weird. I have to keep telling myself, "This is how it's *supposed* to be." I'm slowly getting used to it and enjoying it very much. His friends can't even believe the crazy experiences I've had, because they're normal too! I feel like I've flipped over to the "Bizarro World" in the Seinfeld episode where everyone is kind and considerate.

It's early to tell where things will end up with Mr. Normal, but I'm excited to find out.

2ND EDITION BONUS MATERIAL

You are one of the lucky ones to have purchased the 2nd edition of "10 Rules to Survive the Internet Dating Jungle" which is full of extra oooey goooey dating goodness! I hope you enjoy the extra information to help you venture back out into the dating jungle. Remember to follow me on social media to have the most up-to-date information as well!

www.facebook.com/datingjungle

www.twitter.com/TaraRRichter

www.twitter.com/datingjungleFL

www.youtube.com/user/DatingJungleBook

www.tampadatingjungle.wordpress.com

www.amazon.com/TaraRichter/e/B00CGKD8FG

WHEN SHOULD YOU NOT BE HONEST WHEN ONLINE DATING?

Now don't get your panties all up in a wad from the title of this section. If you have read my books and seen my internet tv show, you know very well I always believe in honesty within your online profiles. However, I do believe there are some circumstances where you should use discrepancy as to what information you put in your profile.

Your online profile is only going to consist of a few paragraphs on information for someone to get to know you well enough to see if they want to go out on a date with you. You want to make sure that it's sweet and to the point so your reader does not get bored. It also needs to reflect you in the best light.

The problem I have seen with some of my clients and even myself, is that if you have a very prestigious type of career, it might attract the wrong kinds of people. For example if you are a wealthy doctor or business owner and make a very nice living for yourself, you may attract the women or men who are looking for a sugar daddy/ sugar momma. If you are ok with that, no problem post pictures of all your flashy cars and houses. However, if you're more down-to-earth and you are looking for a partner who values you for your personality and not your wallet, make sure you are leading with the right foot.

If you are a man and keep getting the "gold diggers" or "trophy wives" and you would rather have a fun lady to go paddle boarding with and fishing, then tone down your profile. It may come off as too flashy and deterring the "real women." For example if you are a wealthy doctor instead of stating that in your profile leave it general & say you are in the medical field. That's a broad category which does describe your career, yet you could be anything from a surgical tech or nurse to running your own practice. Concentrate on describing your hobbies and fun stuff you like to do in your bio to attract women with similar interests. When you get to know someone a few dates in and you know they might be someone you want to go the distance with, then tell them your exact position. Most women wouldn't be too upset, it would be more of a nice surprise. Then you can explain you have difficulties with only getting the "gold digging" girls and you were only trying to avoid that by making sure she likes you for what on the inside.

On the flip side with attracting people that only want you for your sexy body and for intimate encounters, don't post photos of you in a bikini or shirtless in underwear. You get what you fish for. Wear clothes that you look good in, not slutty. Cover up your boobs and abs unless that's the kind of attention you're looking for. Women if you post photos of yourselves half naked, cleavage out & kissy faces, then don't be surprised with the sexual requests you get. Post photos of you dressed nicely, suit or dresses like a classy lady would. Don't give up the goods to early on. With that being said, some women or men will get replies for sex even when they are wearing a turtle neck, if you have a very attractive face. Those people you can just ignore. Dry to dress to impress the type of person you ultimately want in your life.

REVIEW OF TINDER DATING APP

The new trend in the single jungle now is dating apps on your smart phone. This is completely different than online dating sites. Where OkCupid has a website and you fill out the profile with all your information and then download the app to read emails. With the dating apps there is no website linked to it. Everything is in the app on your phone.

You download the app from the iTunes store then install it on your iPhone and login with your Facebook account. (Yes, you must have FB to use Tinder.) It populates a little bit of info from your FB in order to create your Tinder account: 5 photos, your name, your tagline and your friend list. I really don't like my friend list being populated into a dating site. My computer programmer friends tell me the reason they do this is because then people know your identity and that you're not a fraud. Yes, I get this, however people can still open up fake FB accounts to link to these sites. It won't show your friend list to potential dates unless you have a friend in common then it will show that person.

So this small bit of information is pulled in to create your Tinder profile. Then Tinder finds your location with GPS and locates potential dates close to you. You can change your preferences for how many miles away, if you're looking for males or females and the age. Speaking of which, I need to change that preference right now. I kept wondering why I was matched up with such young guys as my screen shot from above, 18? I'm 35 jeeze. Ok, well apparently the age selector doesn't work well. I just switched it to 30-42 & all my matches are still coming up 21, 23?? Does this mean Tinder is not made for middle aged people?

Ok so now to get a date! What you do is play a game. People's photos pop up and you either click the **X** button under their pic for NO you don't like them or the heart button for YES you do like them. It then shuffles through the photos like a deck of cards. Almost like dating Russian roulette. If you click yes on someone and they have also clicked yes, then you have a match & it throws them into another page where you can initiate a chat session with each other.

It seems they are copying the concept of Face Smash from Mark Zuckerberg when he breached security at Harvard University to create the game where college students would rate other students based on their photos. This is the same concept, yet you either say you like them or not. The app is very superficial as you basically have no details other than photos, name & age.

I have yet to meet anyone in person from this app. I have chatted with a few guys from Tinder. However, Tinder does not pull your location from Facebook, so when I look at their "card" I have no idea where they live? For instance I matched with a guy and he asked if I lived in FL, well yea? I thought it did it by location I told him. He responded yes, but he travels so he pulled up Orlando when he was there. I discovered he lives in Mississippi. So no chance we are meeting in person. All the other potential matches I have for some reason live about an hour and a half away. I don't like that because I don't want to start a long distance relationship with someone, so that's a waste of time in my opinion. Been there, done that & got the t-shirt for a LDR (long distance realtionship.)

I've played the game a few times, yet then I get bored. I guess I need a little bit more interaction versus being a monkey clicking on pictures. Personally this really isn't the app for me. It seems more like a hookup app. As when you move your location it's going to pull up people in that area. So is this meant for one nighters or meeting within hours of liking someone's photo? Because I'm not that kind of girl. I want to get to someone a little bit before meeting up.

I don't know if anyone else has had success with Tinder Dating app? Any marriages blossomed? Probably too soon to tell. Yet I rate it 2 out of 5 stars. I need a little more than pretty pictures to keep me entertained.

REVIEW OF LOCK N' KEY EVENTS

I was a sponsor for a local Lock n' Key event in Tampa. I had never attended one of these events, but jumped at the chance to be a sponsor for one. There were about 100 people who attended that night. It was a little bit chilly outside in Florida, yet that didn't seem to damper anyone's mood.

The concept of the Lock n' Key event is that the women get a lock and the men get a key. Then you go around and test your locks n keys to see which ones open. If you lock and key are a match you both get a raffle ticket at the end of the night. You can also exchange your lock/ key for new ones. So after you have tested all the locks, you get a new key and more chances to win more prizes.

193

It's a great concept as an ice-breaker to speak to men and women. I guess these events were around many years ago and are now just making a comeback. I had a great time talking to people and it seemed less awkward versus some of the Match Stir events. It gives you a reason to go up and talk to someone. If your lock doesn't work and you're not really into the person, you can politely excuse yourself to go try someone else lock.   Plus the more locks you open the more chance you have at winning prizes!

My experience from attending Match Stir, POF Hook-a-Fish & Lock-n-Key Events; I like the Lock-n-Key the best. The quality of people was much better, the vibe was good and the mood was overall positive. I had a blast & I think you will too!

Events run from $22-$32 per person. They usually have them about once a month. You can sign up on www.lockandkeyevents.com and find an event near you!

REVIEW OF OK CUPID'S CRAZY DATE APP

The OkCupid's dating app has not been around for that long. Apparently dating apps for smart phones are the new wave of the dating world.

You can download the app for free in the iTunes store. I'm not sure if it is available for other smart phone devices since I'm an avid apple person. Which ever way you get it, you must still have an account already created within OkCupid's regular website. Once you download the app, log in with your account information and it will ask you what dates you are available to go on a date. Then it asks you a local establishment that you would like to meet your blind date at. It will then search the system to match you with a date.

This app is called Crazy Blind Date for a reason. It doesn't really show you a photo of your date. It takes your primary photo, or another one you choose and scrambles it. So you can only see bits and pieces of your date. I'm not sure if I like that feature or not. Could be a hit or miss.

Once the app finds you a match for your date night, then chat is available so you can set up logistics. Hard to find a scrambled face in the bar. So far I have not been set up with anyone as of yet. I put it out there, yet the app keeps saying there are no dates available. It could be the day of the week or possibly that many people are signed up yet utilizing the app. At this time it did have about 130 reviews in the iTunes store, so not sure how many people have downloaded it and in what locations. So that could be an issue until it catches on. Still have not found a crazy blind date as of yet to go out with. Yet I'm not too keen on meeting someone in person that I have no idea who they are. It's bad enough when I *do* know what they look like. Maybe messing the face up would get people together who normally wouldn't. Not sure but I haven't found anyone else brave enough to test out this app either.

REVIEW OF TWINE FLIRTING APP

Apparently this is an app for flirting. It claims to be a mobile wingman. Twine says it connects you with people nearby that share similar interests with you, and gives you interesting things to talk about. You down load it from iTunes & link your Facebook account. It populates your profile picture, likes, interests & hobbies. However, I do not have all my likes and dislikes on my Facebook profile, so that feature is limited.

When you open the app it asks you to find a new twine. After clicking the button it searches for someone close in your area through (I'm assuming) the GPS coordinates on your phone. Since I was testing this out while I was staying in Treasure Island, FL yet I live in Palm Harbor, but it populated Treasure Island as my nearby point of reference.

It then finds a "twine" for you & opens up a chat window to exchange messages or flirt. The only thing is when you click on the person's profile you've matched with, their photo is blurred? I don't know about you, but I don't want to flirt with someone unless I know what they look like. It seems these so called dating apps are revealing less and less information about a person. I don't see how this is a good thing? It really makes the process more difficult. If I'm not even physically attracted to you and don't know how old you are, then there's no way in hell I'm going to flirt with you. I'm sorry but that's attraction 101. It would be nice to think we're fascinated by people on common Interest alone, but that's not reality. But in order to be in a relationship there has to be a physical interest as well.

You can flirt with a blurry photo or you can ask them to reveal themselves. If they choose to reveal their identity, their picture becomes clear along with their first name. That's about all the information you have other than their hobbies. Twine says this is the benefit of their app that it keeps you anonymous. Isn't it kind of hard to get to know an anonymous person? That just creeps me out talking to someone that you can't even see who they are.

The reviews within iTunes on this app is about 2.5 out of 5 stars. I would probably give it a 1.5, I want to know more about someone before I decide to meet them in person or talk to them. That's the whole weeding out process online. The more "in person" weeding out takes a lot more time out of your day, which we keep getting less and less of. Let's make it easier, not harder to date. This method is like picking a person out of a line up while blind folded and hoping they are the one for you.

REVIEW OF LULU APP

While watching E! one night, they discussed this new app called Lulu for women to rate their ex-boyfriends and to find out about potential dates. I immediately downloaded it to see what the fuss was about.

It makes you sign in with Facebook which I don't really like. Why do all new apps and programs make you sign in with Facebook? If you don't have a FB account you can't do hardly anything anymore. Anyway, so reluctantly I let them access my Facebook page. It then populated all the men who are my FB friends onto a scrolling wall. Then other random guys showed up here and there. It allows you to rate guys and put comments good or bad on them anonymously

The app is a good idea and I understand the concept, the few things I do not like about it is that I can only see guys that are my FB friend list. Um ok... well if they're on my list I already know about them! I don't add random weirdoes, not often anyway. If you try to search a guy's name it won't pull up unless, you guessed it, they're on Facebook! Really irritating.

If I'm looking to find dirt on a potential date he's not going to be on any of my social media sites. So basically I can't find him on their app. The other thing is even when you do write and review comments it's all by hash tag. I don't get this? Why hash tags? Does that make their profile pull up in twitter? So example for one man's review would look like this:

#MeanToMyDog, #KinkyInTheRightWays, #Rebel,#RespectsWomen, #GlassHalfFull, #OneWomanMan, #MothersLoveHim, #WritesLoveSongs, #WillSeeRomComs, #MakesMeLaugh, #SweetThreads, #CleansUpGood, #OpensDoors, #CheaperThanABigMac,#FriendZone, #Mama'sBoy, #NoGoals, #NoComment, #DrinksTheHaterade, #ManChild, #JustFriends, #ADD, #SketchyCallLog, #PerfectForMySister, #StillLovesHisEx

I don't know call me old fashioned, but I think that's just too damn hard to read! Then apparently you can add guys from your email or some other stuff, but then they have to create a profile. Why would they want to do that and subject themselves to scrutiny?

I really don't get what all the hype is about in regards to this. If I could search potential dates that were NOT in my Facebook contacts then it would be kinda cool. Oh I forgot to say if I add girlfriends on the app, their guy FB friends get populated into my feed as well. Yet if I was going to go out on a date with a girlfriends friend, I would just ask her about him. So with that being said and the fact I can't read the comments well, my review of Lulu is #epic-fail.

"10 Rules to Survive the Internet Dating Jungle"

ABOUT THE AUTHOR

Tara Richter is an author and publisher. Her first series was three books in "The Dating Jungle." She was featured on CNN, ABC, Daytime TV & FOX. Tara was 2013 Tampa Bay Biz Woman of the Year Finalist, nominee for Tampa Bay's Up & Coming Businesses and nominee for Iconic Woman of the Year 2015. Her books have also been featured on the BBC reality TV series, "Almost Royal."

Tara was a Dating Coach for three years utilizing the methods in her Dating Jungle books. After publication of all her works, she then opened her own publishing company, Richter Publishing LLC (RichterPublishing.com). She soon discovered her true talents were actually helping others tell their stories and share them with the world.

Her company has now published over 30 books in just the last few years. Eight of them reaching Amazon Best Seller status as well as Amazon HOT NEW Releases.

Her list of clients reach all over the World including authors such as Anthony Amos, International Franchising Mogul & Celebrity Entrepreneur, Kevin Harrington, Shark from ABC's "Shark Tank" with their joint book, "How to Catch a Shark."

Richter Publishing has streamlined the complex writing and publishing industry so anyone can become a published author in just a few weeks!

Contact Tara Richter for any speaking engagements, television, or radio shows at http://richterpublishing.com/contact-us/.

RICHTER PUBLISHING